CW01656390

SONGS OF FELLOWSHIP

songs of fellowship

VOLUME FOUR

LARGE PRINT WORDS EDITION

KINGSWAY MUSIC
EASTBOURNE

26–28 Lottbridge Drove, Eastbourne, East Sussex, BN23 6NT, UK.
First published 2008

ISBN 978-1-842913-82-6

Book design by Bookprint Creative Services for
KINGSWAY COMMUNICATIONS LTD
Lottbridge Drove, Eastbourne BN23 6NT, UK.
Printed in Great Britain

1691

Paul Oakley

A FATHER TO THE FATHERLESS,
My shelter from the storm;
My fountain in the wilderness,
My refuge and my rock.
High King of love, God of all grace,
Perfect in power and strong to save;
You have become my hiding place,
My ever-faithful God.

A lover to the loveless,
Defender of the weak;
The healer of all brokenness,
Restorer of my dreams.
High King of love, God of all grace,
Perfect in power and strong to save;
You have become my all in all,
My comfort and my peace.

My substitute, my sacrifice,
My perfect, spotless Lamb;
My risen Lord, my gift of life,
My Saviour and my friend.
High King of love, God of all grace,
Perfect in power and strong to save;
You have become my righteousness,
My glory and my song.

1692

Godfrey Birtill

AFTER I'VE DONE EVERYTHING, I will stand;
With my eyes on my King of kings, I will stand.
I will stand: I will stand in confidence
To see the Lord's deliverance.
Yes, I will stand.

I will stand: of this I'm absolutely sure,
I'll see the goodness of the Lord.
Yes, I will stand.

Because I'm standing with Jesus,
I am standing with my King.
Because I'm standing with Jesus,
I am standing with my King.

Even in the darkest days, I will stand
And bring a sacrifice of praise, I will stand.
I will stand: no matter what is thrown at me,
I'll stand against the devil's schemes.
Yes, I will stand.
I will stand: upright and undisturbed,
Unafraid I'm standing firm,
Yes, I will stand.

Stand, and I will stand with You. *(x3)*
Stand!
(Repeat)

1693

Sue Rinaldi

ALL AROUND YOUR THRONE
There are angels singing.
And all around Your world
There are voices singing.

Holy, holy, holy is the Lord.
Holy, holy, holy is the Lord.

All around Your throne
There are praises rising.
And all around Your world
Men and women rising, singing.

All around Your throne
Holy ground is burning.
And all around Your world
There is faith returning.

From a whisper to a loud shout,
The sound of freedom will ring out.
And we say, 'Yes, Lord, we are ready
To be a living sacrifice.'
(Repeat)

1694 Graham Kendrick & Paul Baloche

ALL CREATION IS A SONG
Waiting to be sung,
All of nature like a prayer
Waiting for a tongue.
For who will give it voice
And make its anthem ring,
Or rise to lead a choir
Of all created things?
Lord, hear Your people sing.

Blessing, honour, glory, power
To creation's King.
Songs of earth and songs of heaven
Join as one to bring
Blessing, honour, glory, power
To creation's King.

All the nations are a song
Waiting to be sung,
Every instrument and voice
Created for the One,
The maker of all things,
The majesty above,

Who brought us back from death
With such a costly love.
What praise could be enough?

All honour, all glory, all power to You.

1695

Paul Oakley & Chris Spring

ALL GLORY TO THE KING of ages.
All glory to the King of kings.
His name is love, His name is Jesus,
Enthroned above in majesty.

Into this world You came to save us,
You bore the cross, You took my sin.
You shone Your light into my darkness,
Unveiled the truth, this mystery.

You are my God, You are my Saviour,
You are the rock on which I stand.

Ever-faithful God, I cling to You.
In every way You've shown
That You are good.
There's no other love compares with You,
Forever strong, forever true.
Ever-faithful God, I cling to You.

You are the end of all my searching,
You pour Your grace on all my need.
Unfailing love, unending mercy
Are found in You, the Prince of Peace.

You are my God…

You are my God, You are my Saviour,
You are the rock on which I stand.
You are my God, You are my Saviour,
Eternal One, the great I Am.

1696

Tré Sheppard

ALL I AM, LORD, all I'll ever be,
Is all for You, Lord, take all of me.
All I have, Lord, all I'll ever see,
Is all for You, Lord, take all of me.

You are worthy, You are wonderful;
For Your glory, take all of me.
You are worthy, You are wonderful;
For Your glory, take all of me.

All I want, Lord, all I'll ever need,
Is all of You, Lord, in all of me.
All I know, Lord, all that I can see,
Is all Your mercy over all of me.

1697

Nathan & Lou Fellingham & busbee

ALL I HAVE AND ALL I AM is Yours;
There's nothing that I have on earth
That doesn't come from You.
I lay aside my pride and worldly worth;
To serve You is the greatest thing
That I could ever do.

For unless You build this house,
I am building it in vain.
Unless the work is Yours,
There is nothing to be gained.
I want something that will stand
When Your holy fire comes;
Something that will last,
And to hear You say 'Well done',
Giving glory to You, Lord,
Glory to You, Lord.

So easy to desire what others have
Instead of seeing all the gifts
That You have given me.
So help me fan the flame which You began,
And burn in me a love for You
That all will clearly see.

1698 Martyn Layzell & busbee

ALL OF ME,
Jesus, You have all of me;
Nothing from You will I keep
Now I am Yours.
All of me,
Jesus, You have all of me;
I will sing beneath Your wings
Now I am Yours.

I'm forever grateful
That You died upon the cross,
A never-failing sacrifice,
Declaring Your true love.
So through Your grace I give You
This living sacrifice:
My offering of worship, my life.

All of me,
Jesus, You have all of me;
Everything to You I bring
Now I am Yours.
All of me,
Jesus, You have all of me;
I surrender as I sing
Now I am Yours.

1699

Dave Clifton & Noel Richards

ALL OF MY LIFETIME
You have been calling,
Though I was far from You.
Even in darkness
Your love has found me;
I could not hide from You.

Search me,
All my deepest longings;
Know me,
All I think and do.
Lead me,
I will walk beside You;
Show me what's good and true.
May I be more like You.

If I should rise on
Wings of the morning,
Fly to a distant shore,
Still You would find me,
Your hand would guide me
Now and forever more.

1700

David Gate

ALL THE KINGS WILL BOW,
Fall down at Your feet,
People of the earth
Will lay down their crowns
And lift up Your name.
We shall come and praise,
Fall down at Your feet,
In the presence of the holy One
We'll fall onto our knees.

With angels and archangels singing,
With the voice of heaven's choir,
Bringing songs of love
That rise up to Your throne.

You are who was, and is,
And is to come:
Jesus, Son of God.
(Repeat)

1701

Paul Oakley

A LOVE SO AMAZING
Has come to save me,
And this love changes everything.
Father, You found me,
Your goodness surrounds me;
I'm Yours for eternity.

And You will always be
The King on the throne;
Now Your praise will always be on my tongue.
No one else could do the things
That You've done in my life.

Your ways are faithful,
Your works are beautiful,
Your word sets the captives free.
Your hand upon me
Heals and restores me,
Your grace fills my every need.

And You will always be
The King on the throne;
Now Your praise will always be on my tongue.
No one else could do the things
That You've done in my life.

There's no greater love
That's ever been shown,
And Your song in me
Just has to be sung.
No one else could do the things
That You've done in my life.

You said if I follow You,
I'll know the truth
And do the things You do.
Yours is the kingdom and the power;
Forever, Lord,
You'll always be my God.

1702

John Newton (1725–1807), John P. Rees (1828–1900),
Edwin O. Excell (1851–1921)
Arr. & add. chorus: Chris Tomlin & Louie Giglio

AMAZING GRACE! how sweet the sound
That saved a wretch like me;
I once was lost, but now am found,
Was blind, but now I see.

'Twas grace that taught my heart to fear,
And grace my fears relieved;
How precious did that grace appear,
The hour I first believed!

My chains are gone,
I've been set free,
My God, my Saviour has ransomed me.
And like a flood His mercy reigns,
Unending love, amazing grace.

The Lord has promised good to me,
His word my hope secures;
He will my shield and portion be
As long as life endures.

The earth shall soon dissolve like snow,
The sun forbear to shine.
But God, who called me here below,
Will be forever mine.

1703

Nathan & Lou Fellingham & busbee

AMAZING LOVE,
Laying down Your glory,
You endured the cross
Instead of us;
Sacrificed Your own life,
Bore the wrath of God.
Jesus, You have paid the price for me,
Made a way to set this sinner free.

Unto You, Lord, I bring my worship,
For You are good, Your love overwhelming.
Hope of the world, Your grace is extended,
Offering life to all who accept it.

Amazing grace,
No way I can earn it;
It's only by Your blood
That I can come.
Trusting in Your mercy,
I'm at peace with God.
Jesus, You have won the victory;
Death has lost its power over me.

1704

Charlie Hall

AND I CAN SEE that my hands are trembling,
I can see that my legs are weak.
I can see that my head is spinning,
But I will overcome.
And I know that my heart is hurting,
And I know that my soul it aches,
And I know that it seems I'm failing,
But I will overcome.

O Lord, I'm strong in You,
O Lord, I'm wise in You.
O Lord, I can see in You,
So I will overcome.
O Lord, I am loved by You,
O Lord, I am free in You.
O Lord, I'm complete in You,
So I will overcome,
I will overcome,
I will overcome.

God, listen to me shout.
I'm so far from anywhere
And I'm calling out:
Lead me, lead me to the rock
That is higher than I.
You're my breath, You're my breath,
You're my very life.
Infinite, holy King
Meets weak and frail: Christ in me.
And I will overcome –
Not by my strength,
But by Your grace and love.

1705

Charlie Hall

AND I WAKE UP, *'cause Your mercy is new*
And it causes me to sing to You.
Yes, I rise up, 'cause Your mercy is new
And it causes me to sing to You.

Praise the Lord, my soul,
And all of my being;
Be my all today
And all that I am seeing.
Keep me close to You,
My heart close to Your speaking.
Father, keep me close, yeah.

And I say today that You
Are true and faithful.
I want Your heart today
And a heart that is grateful.
And in my weakness, Lord,
I know You will sustain me.
Oh, restrain me, God, please.

1706

John Hartley & Gary Sadler

AND WE SING:
You are the Lord, You are glorious.
And we sing:
Your kingdom will reign on the earth
For all time.
And we sing:
Praise to our God the victorious.
Nobody, nobody, nobody else is like You.

Full of mercy, rich in kindness;
God so holy, God so good.
King of glory, shining brightly,
You're majestic, so beautiful.

Man of sorrows, joy of heaven,
Broke the power over us.
Lost in wonder to a Saviour –
Found forever by Your cross!

1707

Darlene Zschech

ANY CROWN I'VE EVER WORN,
I lay it down.
Any praise I've ever gained,
I give it all to You.
For there's nothing in this world
That can compare,
For You alone are worthy,
You alone are worthy.

You are near to all who call
Upon Your name;
Ever-giving, ever-loving,
You remain the same.
For You open up Your hand
And satisfy;
I give You all the glory,
I give You all the glory.

You are worthy, O Lord, of all honour;
You are worthy to receive all praise.
In Your presence I live,
And with all I have to give
I will worship You.

I will worship You, honour You,
Glorify Your holy name.
(Repeat)

1708

Johnny Parks

ARISE, FOR THE GLORY OF THE LORD
Rests upon us now;
Come and sing His praise.
Arise, You're the everlasting light,
Flooding through my night;
I will sing Your praise.

The Lord is our mighty Redeemer,
He gives us love instead of anger.
The gates of our heart are open to You now.

My Redeemer, I will praise You,
My soul will arise, arise!

Arise, sorrow will soon end,
The Lord has heard our prayers;
Come and sing His praise.

Arise, arise, arise, my soul! *(x3)*
Arise!

1709

Darlene Zschech

A SAVIOUR ON A HILL,
Dying for my shame.
Could this be true?
Defies the world I see.
Yet this is all my heart was longing for:
To know You, my Lord,
To know You, Lord.

For You deserve, You deserve,
You deserve all the praise.
You deserve, You deserve,
You deserve all the praise.

The heavens wept for You,
The earth cried out,
'Could He be the One?'
For You so loved the world
You gave Your only Son
To say I love you so,
Oh, how I love you so.

And all humanity
Aches to find
This beautiful love You give.
We come to You again
To offer up our lives
To worship You alone,
To worship You alone.

Hallelujah to the King.
Hallelujah, we will sing forever.
(Repeat)

1710

Evan Rogers

AS FAR AS THE EAST is from the west,
So far have my sins been removed.
You've paid my unpayable debt;
Forgiven, I stand before You.
I'm justified because You died
And shed Your blood for all my sin.
Your sacrifice was the price
That has bought my redemption.

What more is there to dance about?
What more is there to shout about?
What more than Your unfailing love?
What more can we rejoice about?
What more can we be glad about?
Your love is better than life.

You beat the unbeatable grave,
You've done what no other could do;
By Your power I will be raised,
And seated in glory with You.
You give me life, I'll never die,
You have become my salvation.
I'm made alive, for I'm in Christ;
Now there's no condemnation.

Yeah, we dance, yes, we dance,
Come on, we dance
Because of His great love.
Yeah, we're gonna shout,
Yes, we shout,
Come on, we shout
Because of His great love.
(Repeat)

1711

Lara Martin (Abundant Life Ministries, Bradford, England)

AS HIGH AS THE HEAVENS are above the earth,
So high are Your ways to mine.
Ways so perfect they never fail me,
I know You are good all the time!

And through the storm, yet I will praise You,
Despite it all, yet I will sing;
Through good or bad, yet I will worship,
For You remain the same King of kings.

You are the voice of hope,
The anchor of my soul.
Where there seems to be no way,
You make it possible.
You are the Prince of Peace,
Amidst adversity
My lips will shout for joy
To You the Most High!

You were the One before time began;
There's nothing beyond Your control.
My confidence, my assurance
Rest in Your unchanging word!

1712

Johnny Parks

AS JONAH RAN, I've run from You;
Like David, I've sinned too.
And as Thomas needed to rest his eyes
Upon Your feet and hands,
I've doubted too, Lord, but here I stand.

You are the lover of my soul. (x4)

O Holy Ghost, come surround
And breathe life into this shroud.
Help me to rise up from my tomb
And find the stone rolled away.
And like a free man I will say:

1713

Paul Baloche & Glenn Packiam

AS MORNING DAWNS and evening fades,
You inspire songs of praise
That rise from earth to touch Your heart
And glorify Your name.

Your name is a strong and mighty tower.
Your name is a shelter like no other.
Your name, let the nations sing it louder,
'Cause nothing has the power to save
But Your name.

Jesus, in Your name we pray,
Come and fill our hearts today.
Lord, give us strength to live for You
And glorify Your name.

1714

Andy Bromley & Chris Bowater

AS THE LIGHT OF THE SUN in the earth,
Let salvation be known.
As the waters cover the sea,
Let Your glory fill the earth.
That every tribe and every tongue
And every people on the earth
Would hear of Your fame,
Hear the sound of Your name.

Lord of the harvest, send out the workers,
Lord of the harvest, we pray, we pray.
Lord of the harvest, send out the workers,
Lord of the harvest, we pray, we pray.
Lord of the harvest, send out the workers
We pray.

Fields are whiter than they have ever been,
But the workers still few.
So, Lord, I give myself to help the reaping,
To gather precious souls to You.

1715

Paul Oakley

ASTOUNDED BY THE MYSTERY:
The King who died for me;
The holy One who took my place,
Your blood has made me clean.
Oh, how I love You, You've won my heart.

Majesty, I'm on my knees,
I'm bowing down before Your throne.
Jesus, this is Your world,
You're reigning now,
Let Your kingdom come,
Your love made known.

The beauty of Your majesty
Yet remains unseen,
But one day You will split the skies
And every eye will see.
Your glory fills the earth,
Great is our God.

Your glory fills the earth, great is our God.
Your glory fills the earth, great is our God,
Great is our God, great is our God,
Great is our God, great is our God.

1716

Brenton Brown & Paul Baloche

AS WE COME INTO YOUR PRESENCE
We remember every blessing
That You've poured out so freely from above.
Lifting gratitude and praises
For compassion so amazing,
Lord, we've come to give You thanks for all You've done.

Because of Your love we're forgiven;
Because of Your love our hearts are clean.
We lift You up with songs of freedom,
Forever we're changed
Because of Your love.

1717

Graham Kendrick

AS WE GATHER, Father, seal us
In the love that knows no fear.
Draw us, heal us, reconcile us;
May there be a place of refuge here:

Who share one living bread,
One Father's love,
One Saviour's grace,
One Spirit's breath;
One holy communion.

No more outcasts, no more strangers,
All dividing walls are down.
Here is love that redefines us,
Dignifies the least and lowest one:

Source of joy, belonging, friendship,
Form Your family likeness here.
Father, Son and Holy Spirit,
That the world may know our God is near:

1718

Joel Houston

A THOUSAND TIMES I'VE FAILED,
Still Your mercy remains.
And should I stumble again,
Still I'm caught in Your grace.
Everlasting,
Your light will shine when all else fails.
Never ending,
Your glory goes beyond all fame.

Your will above all else
My purpose remains:
The art of losing myself
In bringing You praise.
Everlasting,
Your light will shine when all else fails.
Never ending,
Your glory goes beyond all fame.

In my heart, in my soul,
Lord, I give You control.
Consume me from the inside out, Lord.
Let justice and praise
Become my embrace,
To love You from the inside out.

Everlasting,
Your light will shine when all else fades.
Never ending,
Your glory goes beyond all fame.

And the cry of my heart is to bring You praise
From the inside out.
Lord, my soul cries out.

1719

Kathryn Scott

AT THE FOOT OF THE CROSS
Where grace and suffering meet,
You have shown me Your love
Through the judgement You received.
And You've won my heart,
Yes, You've won my heart.

Now I can trade these ashes in for beauty,
And wear forgiveness like a crown.
Coming to kiss the feet of mercy,
I lay every burden down
At the foot of the cross.

At the foot of the cross
Where I am made complete,
You have given me life
Through the death You bore for me.
And You've won my heart,
Yes, You've won my heart.

1720

Charlie Hall, Kendall Combes,
Dustin Ragland & Brian Bergman

BEAUTIFUL ARE THE WORDS
Spoken to me.
Beautiful is the One
Who is speaking.

Come in close,
Come in close and speak.
Come in close,
Come closer to me.

And the power of Your words
Are filled with grace and mercy.
Let them fall on my ears
And break my stony heart.
(Repeat)

Come in close,
Come in close and speak.
God, come in close,
Come closer to me.
(Repeat)

1721

Mark Beswick & Howard Francis

BE CAREFUL FOR NOTHING,
But with prayer and supplication,
And don't forget thanksgiving,
Make your request unto the Lord.
(Repeat)

Cast all your burdens,
Every one of your cares,
And the God of our salvation will deliver you.
Cast all your burdens
On the Lord and give Him thanks,
For He promised in His word
He will deliver you.

1722 Andy Smith

BEFORE CREATION'S TIME
Majestically You reign,
You patent Your design
On all that You have made.
Creator God, breathe life in us.

We took eternal life
And traded it for dust,
Your perfect sacrifice
Has bought it back for us;
You hold salvation in Your hands.

You turned my ashes into beauty,
Turned my sorrow into joy.
Breathe life, breathe life.
You take these dry bones,
Make them stand,
Put a promise in my hand.
Breathe life, breathe life.

The idols of this world
Will fade to shades of grey,
When marked against the One
Who is the only way,
Bright shining sun that lights my path.

Wonderful, marvellous,
You make all things new.
I was dead, now I'm alive,
All because of You.
So I will go and tell the world
How great You are.

1723

Chris Tomlin, Stephan Sharp & Ed Cash

BEFORE THE DAY,
Before the light,
Before the world revolved around the sun,
God on high
Stepped down into time,
And wrote the story of His love for everyone.
He has filled our hearts with wonder
So that we always remember:

You and I are made to worship,
You and I are called to love,
You and I are forgiven and free.
When you and I embrace surrender,
When you and I choose to believe,
Then you and I will see who we were meant to be.

All we are
And all we have
Is all a gift from God that we receive.
Brought to life,
We open our eyes
To see the majesty and glory of the King.
He has filled our hearts with wonder
So that we always remember:

Even the rocks cry out,
Even the heavens shout,
At the sound of His holy name.
So let every voice sing out,
Let every knee bow down;
He's worthy of all our praise.

1724

Keith & Kristyn Getty & Stuart Townend

BEHOLD THE LAMB who bears our sins away,
Slain for us: and we remember
The promise made that all who come in faith
Find forgiveness at the cross.
So we share in this bread of life,
And we drink of His sacrifice,
As a sign of our bonds of peace
Around the table of the King.

The body of our Saviour, Jesus Christ,
Torn for you: eat and remember
The wounds that heal, the death that brings us life,
Paid the price to make us one.
So we share in this bread of life,
And we drink of His sacrifice,
As a sign of our bonds of love
Around the table of the King.

The blood that cleanses every stain of sin
Shed for you: drink and remember
He drained death's cup that all may enter in
To receive the life of God.
So we share in this bread of life,
And we drink of His sacrifice,
As a sign of our bonds of grace
Around the table of the King.

And so with thankfulness and faith
We rise to respond and to remember
Our call to follow in the steps of Christ
As His body here on earth.
As we share in His suffering
We proclaim: Christ will come again!
And we'll join in the feast of heaven
Around the table of the King.

1725

Keith & Kristyn Getty

BENEATH THE CROSS OF JESUS,
I find a place to stand
And wonder at such mercy
That calls me as I am.
For hands that should discard me
Hold wounds which tell me 'Come.'
Beneath the cross of Jesus
My unworthy soul is won.

Beneath the cross of Jesus
His family is my own;
Once strangers chasing selfish dreams,
Now one through grace alone.
How could I now dishonour
The ones that You have loved?
Beneath the cross of Jesus
See the children called by God.

Beneath the cross of Jesus,
The path before the crown,
We follow in His footsteps
Where promised hope is found.
How great the joy before us –
To be His perfect bride.
Beneath the cross of Jesus
We will gladly live our lives.

1726

Nick Herbert & John Peters

BEYOND THESE PRESENT SUFFERINGS
Future glory waits.
Keep my heart remembering
In each desert place…

That You rejoice from heights above
To quiet my soul with Your great love;
To hear the sound of Your delight,
You're singing over me.

Such a healing harmony,
Tune my heart to hear
Your unbroken melody,
The truth that You are near...

Beautiful in my sight,
You're beautiful in my sight.
I am Yours and You are mine.
(Repeat)

This is the song of songs
To which each heart is drawn,
And You're singing over me.

1727

Tim Hughes, Rob Hill & Jon Mann-Smith

BIGGER THAN THE AIR I BREATHE,
Deeper than the ocean deep,
Higher than the stars above, You are.
Brighter than the blazing sun,
Louder than the screaming crowd,
Stronger than the power of death, You are.

In the heavens, on the earth,
There is no one like You, God,
And these words are not enough
To tell of who You are.
Who can know the mind of God?
Who can understand Your ways?
And these words are not enough
To tell of Your great name.

Your love can melt the hardest heart,
Your words can bring the dead to life:
Nothing is impossible for You.
Awesome God, humble King,
You terrify yet welcome in;
Your glory echoes all around the world.

You, You, You –
There's always You, You, You:
Unbreakable, unshakable, unbeatable.
You, You, You –
There's always You, You, You.
Take the world but give me You,
Lord Jesus, You.

1728

Stuart Townend

BLESSÈD SPIRIT OF THE KING,
Of grace and love the author,
Work repentance deep within
And bend me at Your altar.
Melt my heart with majesty,
Then show my ruined self to me;
Teach me to more clearly see
Your might and will to save me.

Here I place without reserve
My soul in faith and meekness,
Trusting in Christ's power and love
To flourish in my weakness.
Cause my days on earth to be,
Through time and through eternity,
A trophy of His victory,
A monument to mercy.

Teach me to behold my God
And trust His power to save me,

Arms outstretched in constant love,
Whose strength will never fail me.
Help me to commune with Him,
Depend and follow after Him,
That through my life His peace will reign
And joy be my companion.

1729

Eoghan Heaslip

BLESSING, HONOUR, GLORY AND POWER
Be to our God forever.
Blessing, honour, glory and power
Be to our God forever.

Hallelujah,
Our Lord God Almighty reigns.
Hallelujah, amen.
Hallelujah,
Our Lord God Almighty reigns.
Hallelujah, amen.

Come and worship, bow before Him,
Your voices join the singing.
(Repeat)

1730

Godfrey Birtill

BLESS THE LORD, O MY SOUL,
And all that is within me.
(Repeat)
Bless His holy name,
Bless His holy name.

He is good, good to us,
And His love endures forever.
(Repeat)

Bless His holy name,
Bless His holy name.

Open wide heaven's gates;
Let the King of glory in.
(Repeat)
Bless His holy name,
Bless His holy name.

1731

Keith & Kristyn Getty

BORN WHERE THE SHADOWS LIE,
To answer every cry of man,
This child who formed all life
Now breathes our breath.
Born where the Father loved,
Born helpless to a mother's arms,
She smoothed the tears upon
The face of God.

Born now with man to dwell,
Our Lord, Immanuel;
Come see the King, the Christ child born to us.
Born now with man to dwell,
Our Lord, Immanuel;
My soul can finally know the God of heaven.

Born with a road ahead,
Alone these blameless feet would tread
The path God chose to walk
Before all time.
Born holding life and death,
Born bearing heaven's wealth of peace
That fills where none can fill
Our living stream.

1732

Paul Oakley

BREATHE ON ME, breath of God.
Breathe on me, breath of God.
Fill my life,
Have my heart,
Breath of God.

Living breath, draw me close,
Face to face, Holy Spirit, have your way.
Living fire, burn inside,
Glorify my Saviour's name,
Lord, I pray,
Breath of God.

1733

Paul Oakley

BREATHTAKING, overwhelming,
Your grace is so astounding.
Here I stand, made alive in You.
Unchanging, never ending,
Your mercy's so surprising.
Here I am, ever loved by You,
Your kindness draws me to You,
Your praise will be my song.

You are glorious, magnificent,
All-powerful,
Everlasting God,
I believe in You.
You are wonderful, the risen One,
So merciful,
Everlasting God,
I will worship You.

You were bruised and You were broken,
Crucified for me, forsaken;
How can I ever thank You, God?
Now risen, now reigning,
My foolish heart You awakened;
Let my life tell of all You've done.
Your love is so far reaching,
Your mercies carry on.

1734

Robert Critchley

CAN A THOUSAND SOULS be won in a day?
Can we win our cities when we fast and pray?
Could our trembling hands bring Your healing grace?
And the words we speak have the power to save?

Our heads are spinning, but our hearts say yes.
You've given us vision, now we face the test.
The words of the prophets are within our grasp
When we risk it all to follow in Your steps.

Our hearts say yes!
Our hearts say yes!

We have prayed for revival flowing from above,
And our lives have been changed by the Father's love.
As Your people rejoice in the oil and the wine,
Will we see a great harvest gathered in our time?

'Cause we are dreamers of impossible dreams,
Walking by faith in what is yet unseen.
Number us, Lord, with those who dare to believe,
That we can live in Your impossible dream.

All things are possible
Through Christ, who strengthens me.
All things are possible

When God says, 'Let it be.'
(Repeat)
When God says, 'Let it be.'

1735

Gareth Robinson

CLAP YOUR HANDS and celebrate,
Sing to God and praise His name.
Shout for joy, for He is good,
His mercy never ends.
Gather here and join as one,
Think on Him and all He's done.
Stir your soul to worship Him,
The King above all kings.

Hallelujah, hallelujah, hallelujah,
His mercy never ends.

God of all gods,
King of all kings,
Lord of all lords –
Give glory to Him.
(Repeat)

1736

Andy Bromley & Chris Donohue

CLOTHED WITH SPLENDOUR AND MAJESTY,
You wear light like a robe,
The heavens from Your sheltering hand unfold;
Awesome God.
You laid the earth on its foundation,
At the sound of Your voice
The mountains and oceans took their places;
Awesome God.

All the earth displays Your glory,
All creation calls Your name;
As all of heaven is standing in awe,
All the nations shout Your praise.

Creation's anthem will rise to You,
All the universe is crying out for You,
In adoration to the holy One,
In higher praises to the awesome God.

1737

Vicky Beeching

COME, ALL WHO ARE WEARY,
Battle-worn and weak.
Come, all of us broken,
Tired and in need.
For I for one am weary,
Lonely and afraid.
So let us run for shelter
In the Saviour's strong embrace.
Come, one and all, let us fall...

Into the everlasting arms.
I'm running into the everlasting arms.
I'm falling into eternity's embrace,
Where I'm safe.
Here my heart has found its resting place.

Here we find our healing
And here we find our peace,
Wrapped in Your unfailing love,
Surrounded by Your peace.
So I for one am letting
All my walls fall down.
In this place of safety,
This child is finally found.
Come, one and all, let us fall...

And I'm finally home,
I'm no longer alone.
You surround me,
All around me with Your love.
(Repeat)

1738

David Crowder

COME AND LISTEN;
Come to the water's edge,
All you who know and fear the Lord.
Come and listen;
Come to the water's edge,
All you who are thirsty, come.

Let me tell you what He has done for me;
Let me tell you what He has done for me,
He has done for you, He has done for us.

Come and listen,
Come and listen to what He's done.
Come and listen,
Come and listen to what He's done.

Praise our God, for He is good. *(x4)*

1739

Andrew Mitchell

COME AND MEET THE LORD,
The Saviour of our souls.
He is like no other,
Like no one else I know.
(Repeat)

O Spirit of the Lord,
Let Your glory fall.
Lord, we cry to You
To move among us all,
That we may dwell in You,
Our lives in one accord.
My heart cries out:
'Spirit of the Lord!'

This is where I come
To lay my burdens down.
Jesus is among us –
This is holy ground.

Crowned with many crowns,
The man of sorrows reigns;
And through His tender mercy
Brings life to me again.

1740

Keith & Kristyn Getty

COME, LET US SING TO THE ONE,
To the Father of life,
Whose light fills the earth like the sun;
Come, tell of the wonders He's done.
Great is the world He has made,
Are the mysteries untold,
Is His measureless power of old;
Come, come let us sing to our God.

To our God, who is able
To strengthen us in His grace
Beyond all we imagine,
Be all glory and praise,
Be all praise.

Come, let us sing to the One,
To the Saviour of life,
Find the fullness of God in the Son;
Come, tell of the wonders He's done.
Wild is the mercy of Christ,
Is the richness of grace,
Is the unending life we embrace;
Come, come let us sing to our God.

Come, let us sing to the One,
To the Spirit of life,
Leading us in the way of the Son;
Come, tell of the wonders He's done.
Strong is the Spirit within,
Is the boldness to speak,
Is the power to run when we're weak;
Come, come let us sing to our God.

1741

Godfrey Birtill

COME, O SPIRIT OF THE FEAR OF THE LORD.
Come, O Spirit of the fear of the Lord,
Through another veil,
To a deeper level,
To foretaste the awe-ful
Beyond what we have known,
To get in line before You,
To walk the way of wisdom.

I want to keep in step with the Holy Spirit,
Keep in step with the Holy Spirit,
Keep in step with the Holy Spirit,
Keep in step with the Holy Spirit.

1742

William C. Dix (1837–1898)
Music: Ian Hannah

'COME UNTO ME, ye weary,
And I will give you rest.'
O blessèd voice of Jesus,
Which comes to hearts oppressed.
It tells of benediction,
Of pardon, grace and peace,
Of joy that hath no ending,
Of love which cannot cease.

'Come unto Me, ye wanderers,
And I will give you light.'
O loving voice of Jesus,
Which comes to cheer the night.
Our hearts were filled with sadness
And we have lost our way.
But morning brings us gladness,
And songs the break of day.

'Come unto Me, ye fainting,
And I will give you life.'
O cheering voice of Jesus,
Which comes to aid our strife.
The foe is stern and eager:
The fight is fierce and long.
But Thou hast made us mighty
And stronger than the strong.

'And whosoever cometh,
I will not cast him out.'
O welcome voice of Jesus,
Which drives away our doubt;
Which calls us very sinners,
Unworthy though we be
Of love so free and boundless,
To come, dear Lord, to Thee.

1743

Matt Redman & Peter Wilson

CONDEMNATION FALLS AWAY,
Never more to call on me,
And I am clean, I am clean.
The powerful work of You in me
Breaks the chains of guilt and shame,
And I go free, I go free.

I take them to Your cross
And leave them there;
Captured by this grace
I'm free at last.

It is the great gift of Your salvation
Working in me,
Working in me.
It is the life-giving taste of heaven
Your kindness revealed,
Your kindness revealed to me.

It's the greatest gift of all. *(x3)*

Your mercy's pouring down on me,
Your mercy's pouring down on me,
And I am clean, yes, I am clean.
Your mercy's pouring down on me,
Your mercy's pouring down on me,
And I go free, yes, I go free.

1744

Mark Tedder

CRIMSON BLOOD, pure as snow,
Freely flowed, freely flowed.
God's compassion came to man,

To the place I stand.
Cruel crown that pierced His head,
Pressed upon the Son of man.
Placed upon His heart our crime,
Because of love, because of love.

Because of love He came, He raised, He gave.
Because of love He came, no shame, no blame.
Because of love He came, no other name.
Because of love, because of His love.

Broken body, lifeless form,
Taken from the cross of scorn.
Anointed shell, encased with care,
Fragranced by a mother's tear.
As the tomb, this hollow grave,
Came to life that very day;
Christ in glory bursting forth
Because of love, because of love.

1745

Keith & Kristyn Getty

CROSS OF JESUS, cross of sorrow,
Where our sinfulness was laid,
Perfect love on You was broken
As the way to God was paved.
Cross of love, the scar of heaven,
Cross of love that heals my soul,
Let me not forget such mercy,
Let me give the life I owe.

Oh, what language shall I borrow
As I praise You, faithful Friend?
How for us You bore our suffering
In Your love, which has no end.

Died that I might be forgiven
By a power not my own.
With His glory set before me,
Cross of Jesus, lead me home.

1746

John Newton (1725–1807) & Tim Hughes

DANCE, DANCE, EVERYBODY DANCE,
Everybody sing, for joy is in this place now.
Dance, dance, everybody dance,
Everybody sing, for joy is in this place now.
And everybody dance now.
And everybody dance now.

Amazing grace, how sweet the sound,
To save a wretch like me;
I once was lost, but now I'm found,
Was blind, but now I see.

Shout, shout, everybody shout,
Everybody scream, for joy is in this place now.
Shout, shout, everybody shout,
Everybody scream, for joy is in this place now.
Yeah, joy is in this place now.
Yeah, joy is in this place now.

1747

Vicky Beeching

DOESN'T MATTER WHAT PEOPLE SAY,
I forget their watching eyes.
I just want to bring to You
My most costly, my most precious,
My most priceless sacrifice.

Extravagant worship,
Total surrender,

Reckless abandon.
I pour out my love,
I pour out myself, Saviour.

Breaking open my thankful heart,
I release its praise perfume.
Here I'll linger, lifting to You
Songs of wonder, songs of worship,
Songs of deepest gratitude.

1748

Simon Goodall

DRAW ME CLOSE, NEVER LET ME GO.
Keep me near, so my heart will know
Unfailing love that comforts me,
Brings peace and calm;
You're ever near.

Draw me close, never let me go.
Keep me near, so my heart will know
The blood You shed, it washes clean
My guilt and shame;
You're ever near.

Draw me close, never let me go.
Keep me near, so my heart will know
All of my days, mercy is free.
Goodness and grace
You have given to me.

1749

Noel & Michelle-John Robinson

EACH DAY I WILL CONTINUALLY PRAISE
For Your goodness, Your mercy and Your grace.
Without Your peace no love remains,
Your word in me declares Your name.

O holy One, we reverence Your name,
Your kingdom come, Your people to save.
Your will on earth be done through me;
Your Spirit leads us to victory.

So I sing and I dance;
Wherever I am I will shout it.

You are good all of the time
And Your mercy endureth.
You are good all of the time
And Your mercy endureth forever.

From the rising to my going down,
My soul rejoices in the love I've found.
Your goodness I just can't explain –
You bring something new each and every day.

Not one minute,
Not one hour,
Not one day
Without Your power.
(Repeat)

1750

Andy Bromley

EARLY IN THE MORNING
I lift my eyes to You,
Early in the morning.
Early in the morning
My song will rise to You,
Early in the morning.

When I awake, I'm still with You,
Thank You, thank You.

From the rising of the sun,
You are near, faithful Friend of mine.
Like the dawning of the day,
New hope will rise;
You are near, faithful Friend of mine.

1751

Simon Brading & Matt Redman

ENDLESS MERCY FALLS DOWN like a flood
Each time I wander astray.
Slow to anger, abounding in love,
I find no end to Your grace.
But I'm found within Your embrace.

Many times have I fallen astray,
Many times have I failed.
Lord, Your mercy has found me
Just as I am, You've turned me around.

East to west is a distance unknown;
In truth they never will meet.
Just as far now I live from my shame,
Removed forever from me;
Now I'll live forgiven and free.

You love me, You cleanse me,
You wash me whiter than the snow.
You catch me, You hold me,
Your love will never let me go.

1752

Matt Redman & Martin Smith

EVEN AS THE WORLD BEGAN,
The stars they sang
And all the angels shouted for joy, shouted for joy.

And looking back through history
Your people they have always had
A song they must sing, a song they must sing.
We are the people of God;
We'll sing Your song here on the earth.

All over the world Your song will resound.
All over the world Your praises ring out.
We're living to see Your name and renown
All over the world.

Young and old, near and far,
There's a place for every heart to join in Your song,
To join in Your song.
Every nation, tribe and tongue
Come together, join as one,
Give glory to God, give glory to God.
We are the people of God;
We'll sing Your song here on the earth.

Great is Your name
And great will be Your song.
Great is Your name
And great will be Your song.
We lift up our hands and pray,
We lift up our hands and pray,
For holy is Your name.

1753

Matt & Beth Redman

EVEN THOUGH I WALK THROUGH THE VALLEY
Of the shadow of death,
Your perfect love is casting out fear.
And even when I'm caught in the middle
Of the storm of this life,
I won't turn back; I know You are near.

And I will fear no evil,
For my God is with me.
And if my God is with me,
Whom then shall I fear?
Whom then shall I fear?

Oh no, You never let go,
Through the calm and through the storm.
Oh no, You never let go,
In every high and every low.
Oh no, You never let go,
Lord, You never let go of me.

And I can see a light that is coming
For the heart that holds on;
A glorious light beyond all compare.
And there will be an end to these troubles,
But until that day comes,
We'll live to know You here on the earth.

Yes, I can see a light that is coming
For the heart that holds on,
And there will be an end to these troubles,
But until that day comes,
Still I will praise You, still I will praise You.
(Repeat)

1754

Vicky Beeching

EVERLASTING GOD,
The years go by, but You're unchanging.
In this fragile world,
You are the only firm foundation.
Always loving, always true,
Always merciful and good, so good.

Yesterday, today and forever,
You are the same, You never change.
Yesterday, today and forever,
You are faithful and we will trust in You.

(Second time)
We will trust in You, we will trust in You.

Uncreated One,
You have no end and no beginning.
Earthly powers fade,
But there is no end to Your kingdom.
Always loving, always true,
Always merciful and good, so good.

Yahweh, God unchanging.
Yahweh, firm foundation.
(Repeat)

1755

Reuben Morgan

EVERY KNEE WILL BOW
And every tongue confess
That Jesus Christ is Lord,
Lord and King.

All glory to Your name,
All honour to Your majesty,
Forever, forever,
All praise to You alone.

Every eye will see
And every heart will know
The beauty of the Lord
In all the earth.

All praise to You alone. *(x4)*

1756

Ed Cash, Jesse Reeves & Chris Tomlin

EVERYONE AROUND THE WORLD,
Hear the joyful sound.
See the heavens open up,
Hear the music coming down.
Nothing's gonna separate us from the Father's love.
I can't help but celebrate,
Because we're not alone.

If God is on our side,
Who can be against us?
If God is on our side,
We won't be afraid.
Though the mountains may fall
And the sky will crumble,
There ain't nothin' gonna stand in our way.

Come on down to the riverside,
Wash it all away.
Leave behind your troubled mind
For an uncloudy day.
Nothing's gonna separate us from the Father's love.
I can't help but celebrate,
Because we're not alone.

1757

Reuben Morgan & Ben Fielding

EVERYONE NEEDS COMPASSION,
Love that's never failing;
Let mercy fall on me.
Everyone needs forgiveness,
The kindness of a Saviour;
The hope of nations.

Saviour,
He can move the mountains,
My God is mighty to save,
He is mighty to save.
Forever,
Author of salvation,
He rose and conquered the grave,
Jesus conquered the grave.

So take me as You find me,
All my fears and failures;
Fill my life again.
I give my life to follow
Everything I believe in;
Now I surrender.

Shine your light
And let the whole world see
We're singing for the glory
Of the risen King, Jesus.
Shine your light
And let the whole world see
We're singing for the glory
Of the risen King.

1758

Andy Bromley

EVERYTHING I HAVE COMES FROM YOU:
Everything I long for
I lay down before You.
Everything I am
I surrender to Your hand:
I give myself,
Bow my knee again.

Acknowledge You, my Lord,
Acknowledge You, King of all;
Acknowledge You,

My Saviour and my God.
(Repeat)
My Saviour and my God.

1759

Marty Sampson, Dylan Thomas & Joel Davies

FALLING ON MY KNEES in worship,
Giving all I am to seek Your face,
Lord, all I am is Yours.

My whole life I place in Your hands,
God of mercy, humbled, I bow down
In Your presence, at Your throne.

I called, You answered,
And You came to my rescue.
And I, I wanna be where You are.

In my life, be lifted high.
In our world, be lifted high.
In our love, be lifted high.
(Repeat)

1760

Verses: Laurence Tuttiet (1825–1897)
Adpt. Matt Redman/Chorus: Chris Tomlin, Louie Giglio & Jesse Reeves

FATHER, LET ME DEDICATE
All this life to Thee,
In whatever worldly state
Thou wilt have me be.
Not from sorrow, pain or care

Freedom dare I claim;
This alone shall be my prayer:
Glorify Thy name.

Be glorified in me,
Be glorified.
Be glorified in me,
Be glorified.

Can a child presume to choose
Where or how to live?
Can a father's love refuse
All the best to give?
Let my glad heart, while it sings,
Thee in all proclaim,
And, whate'er the future brings,
Glorify Thy name.

1761

Martyn & Emily Layzell

FATHER, O MY FATHER,
From the shadows You have lifted me,
Placed me on Your shoulders,
Took my burdens; You have carried me.
Knowing You has become my life.
Only You are my heart's desire.

I'm longing to know You
More than anything, more than anything.
I want just to love You
More than anything, more than anything.

Father, Abba Father,
You are with me when I feel alone.
Lead me in green pasture,
By still water; You restore my soul.
Knowing You has become my life.
Only You are my heart's desire.

I come to You with everything,
There's nothing more that I can bring.
This simple song my offering;
I love You more than anything.
(Repeat)
I love You more than anything.

1762 Stuart Townend & Keith Getty

FATHER, WE HAVE SINNED
In word, and deed, and thought,
Through ignorance, through weakness,
Through deliberate fault.
We've sinned against our neighbours
And against You, Lord,
Yet we are truly sorry
And we turn to You once more.

Father of the nations,
You who bless the poor,
We're servants of the endless want
And drive for more.
We've made our greed a virtue
While the children starve;
Come, change our joy to sorrow,
Till our lives reflect Your heart.

1763 David Lyon

FATHER, YOU ARE HOLY
And before You we will fall.
Reign, Lord, as in heaven,
Bring Your kingdom to this place.

This will be our prayer, Father,
This will be our prayer.
Asking as You taught us to;
This will be our prayer.

Father, our provider,
In Your goodness meet our need.
Free us and restore us,
Make us willing to forgive.

Lead us from temptation,
Come and save us from all sin.
Glory and all power,
Lord, forever will be Yours.

1764

Robert Critchley

FATHER, YOUR LOVE is a faithful love,
Enduring and never-failing love.
Throughout the ages steady and true,
And the dawn of each day
Brings Your mercies new.
And I will put my trust in You;
Father, Your love is faithful.
(Repeat)

So keep me in Your love today,
Take my hand and lead the way,
And let my words and life convey,
Father, Your love is faithful.

Great is Your faithfulness, *(x3)*
My God and Father.
(Repeat)

1765

Inspired by the Moravian Hymn
Godfrey Birtill

FEAR NOT, O LITTLE FLOCK.
The foe who madly seeks to overthrow
Will come crashing down.
Dread not his rage and power;
His seeming triumph over all God's saints
Lasts a little hour.
True as God's word is true,
Not earth nor hell and all its crew
Against us shall prevail.
Our victory just cannot fail.

Rise up! Rise up!
Rise up! Rise up! Rise up!
(Repeat)

Fear not, O little flock.
Be sharp! Be strong!
Your cause to God belongs.
Fix your eyes and pray,
Stand with the God of peace;
He'll soon crush Satan
Underneath your feet
In this your battle day.
Lord Jesus, grant our prayer;
Great Captain, now Your arm make bare.
As Your sword sweeps the skies,
We'll see salvation here arise.

So hold on! Hold on!
Hold on! Hold on! Hold on!
(Repeat)
Keep your hand on that plough!
Hold on!
(Repeat)

1766

Geraldine Latty

FIRST IN POURING OUT YOUR LOVE upon us
Before we asked.
First in showing that a King could save us,
Not holding back.
You are first in all the praise of heaven,
First where people know that they're forgiven.

Jesus, the first to rise again.
Jesus, the One who holds all things together,
Together.
Jesus, we lift our praise to You.
Jesus, we say that You are King forever,
Forever.
The one and only, first and last, Jesus!

First in speaking light into the darkness,
Creation wakes.
First in breathing life into our weakness,
Your image placed.
You are first, and all creation's longings
Will one day erupt in joyful song.

First in showing radical redemption
To the lost and least.
First in bringing hope and transformation
To the poor and weak.
First to call us to a way of dying
That in You becomes a life worth living.

1767

Rex Allchurch

FOREVER FAITHFUL, FOREVER TRUE,
Forever loving, forever You will be.
(Repeat)

More than enough for me,
More than I can see,
More than I conceive, You will be.
(Repeat)

And I'll be Yours,
Keep You as centre,
Serving no other, only You.
And You'll be mine,
Forever and ever,
I'll keep You as centre, only You.

1768

Dave Bilbrough

FOR EVERY CHILD that stands abused,
For all the lonely and confused,
For those who suffer for the truth,
Hear our prayer.

For those who mourn the ones they knew,
Who stand accused for loving You,
Lord, we long to see You move;
Hear our prayer.

Hear our prayer, hear our prayer,
Hear our prayer, hear our prayer.

For all who bear the marks of hate,
Who are wounded for Your sake,
These are champions of the faith;
Hear our prayer.

For those who weep, for those who grieve,
For those in need we intercede.

Console the powerless and the weak,
The ones denied a right to speak;
Bring Your comfort and release;
Hear our prayer.

1769

Noel Richards & Tim Sherrington

FOR THE WORLD THAT HE HAS MADE,
Praise the Lord.
Stars and universe ordained,
Praise the Lord.
All creation He sustains;
Praise the Lord in whom we live and breathe.

Holy, holy, holy is the Lord.
Holy, holy, holy is the Lord.

For the world that He has saved,
Praise the Lord.
For the life He freely gave,
Praise the Lord.
Sin and death He overcame;
Praise the Lord in whom we live and breathe.

God who is and is to come,
Praise the Lord.
First and last and living One,
Praise the Lord.
Voices join with heaven's song;
Praise the Lord in whom we live and breathe.

Join with heaven's song,
Praise the Lord.
Join with heaven's song,
Praise the Lord.
(Repeat)

1770

Matt Weeks, Geraldine Latty & Matt Redman

FOR YOU HAVE BEEN WITH US,
Graced us with Your presence.
Cloud by day and fire by night,

You have never left us.
And You have been for us a firm foundation.
And You have been for us a God that we can trust.

Great is our Lord,
Mighty in power;
All the earth will sing.
Great is our Lord,
Faithful forever;
You alone are God.

For You will lead us on into all You promised.
Through the night and through the storm,
Always leading Your people.
And You will be for us grace sufficient.
And You will be for us all we'll ever need.

So, Father, be with us and send us in Your power.
Today we choose again
To follow and obey You.
For You have been to us a perfect Father.
And You have been to us dependable and true.

You are good, Lord, gracious in all You do.
You are good, Lord, mighty in all Your power.
You are good, Lord, wisdom beyond compare.
You are good, Lord,
Loving us when we don't deserve Your love,
Loving us when we don't deserve Your love.

1771

Joel Houston

FOUND LOVE BEYOND ALL REASON;
You gave Your life, Your all for me,
And called me Yours forever.
Caught in the mercy fallout,

I found hope, found life,
Found all I need.
You're all I need.

The time has come
To stand for all we believe in,
So I for one am gonna give my praise to You.

Today, today it's all or nothing;
All the way
Praise goes out to You.
Yeah, all the praise goes out to You.
Today, today I live for one thing:
To give You praise
In everything I do.
Yeah, all the praise goes out to You.

All we are is Yours,
And all we're living for
Is all You are,
Is all that You are.

1772

Brian Doerksen & Matt Unruh

FROM EVERLASTING TO EVERLASTING
You are God.
From everlasting to everlasting
You are God.

In holiness You stand secure
Through culture's shifting sands,
Unchanged by all the vanities of man.
And as the nations rise and fall
Your sovereignty remains.
You are, You are,
You are the one true God.

In faithfulness Your love extends
Through times of turbulence,
Adopting those who call upon Your name.
And every generation joins
In songs of grateful praise.
You are, You are,
You are the one true God.

Eternal, (Eternal)
Immortal, (Immortal)
Invisible (Invisible) God.
(Repeat)

1773

Rex Allchurch

FROM THE ANCIENT DAYS until today
And the days beyond,
You'll always reign in power.
From the day I was born until today
And the days beyond,
You'll always be my Father.

And Your love will last forever,
And Your goodness will never fail.

When the world was made until today
And the days beyond,
You'll always reign in majesty.
From the north to south and east to west,
From the deep to high,
You'll always be the maker.

Now and forever
You reign in all splendour.
(Repeat)

1774

Keith Getty & Stuart Townend

FROM THE BREAKING OF THE DAWN
To the setting of the sun,
I will stand on every promise of Your word.
Words of power, strong to save,
That will never pass away;
I will stand on every promise of Your word.
For Your covenant is sure,
And on this I am secure:
I can stand on every promise of Your word.

When I stumble and I sin,
Condemnation pressing in,
I will stand on every promise of Your word.
You are faithful to forgive,
That in freedom I might live,
So I stand on every promise of Your word.
Guilt to innocence restored;
You remember sins no more,
So I'll stand on every promise of Your word.

When I'm faced with anguished choice
I will listen for Your voice,
And I'll stand on every promise of Your word.
Through this dark and troubled land
You will guide me with Your hand
As I stand on every promise of Your word.
And You've promised to complete
Every work begun in me,
So I'll stand on every promise of Your word.

Hope that lifts me from despair,
Love that casts out every fear
As I stand on every promise of Your word.
Not forsaken, not alone,
For the Comforter has come,
And I stand on every promise of Your word.

Grace sufficient, grace for me,
Grace for all who will believe;
We will stand on every promise of Your word.

1775 Laura Story; additional lyrics by Jesse Reeves

FROM THE HIGHEST OF HEIGHTS
To the depths of the sea,
Creation's revealing Your majesty.
From the colours of fall
To the fragrance of spring,
Every creature unique
In the song that it sings.
All exclaiming:

Indescribable, uncontainable,
You placed the stars in the sky,
And You know them by name:
You are amazing, God.
All-powerful, untamable;
Awestruck, we fall to our knees
As we humbly proclaim:
You are amazing, God.

Who has told every lightning bolt
Where it should go,
Or seen heavenly storehouses
Laden with snow?
Who imagined the sun
And gives source to its light,
Yet conceals it to bring us the coolness of night?
None can fathom.

Indescribable, uncontainable,
You placed the stars in the sky,
And You know them by name:

You are amazing, God.
Incomparable, unchangeable,
You see the depths of my heart
And you love me the same;
You are amazing, God.

1776

Paul Baloche & Matt Redman

FROM THE RISING OF THE SUN
Till the sun goes down,
Let the name of the Lord be praised.
From the rising of the sun
Till the sun goes down,
Let the name of the Lord be praised.
From the sky to the depths,
From the east to the west,
We give You praise.

We've gathered to worship,
Becoming a choir to sing Your praise.
Lifting our voices,
Joining our hearts in this house today.
People of God, in the power of God,
For the kingdom of God we sing.

We're gathered to go out;
To cities and towns we'll take Your name.
Into the nations,
Shining Your light in the darkest place.
People of God, in the power of God,
For the kingdom of God we live.

1777

Andrew Mitchell

FROM THE RISING SUN to its setting place
We will sing as one, blessèd be Your name.

You have placed our feet on a solid rock
That we won't let go or be shaken from.

Lord of all the earth,
King of love, in praise I sing.
Faithful are Your works
And glorious Your name,
Lord of all the earth.

I was laid in dust, weary in my soul,
Tired and overcome, full of sorrows old.
But You heard my cry, though I'd walked astray;
Still You offered life and new hope again.

So to You, O Lord, and Your name always,
We give thanks to You, King of endless grace;
For Your love endures and Your power remains;
There is only one Name above all names!

And we sing hallelujah,
Great is the name of our Lord.
We sing hallelujah,
Great is the name of our Lord.
And we sing hallelujah,
Great is the name of our Lord.
Yes, we sing hallelujah,
Great is the name of our Lord.
And sing once more,
Lord of all the earth. *(x5)*

1778

David Crowder

FROM WHEREVER SPRING ARRIVES to heal the ground,
From wherever searching comes,
The look itself,
A trace of what we're looking for,
So be quiet now and wait.

The ocean is growing,
The tide is coming in; here it is.

Here is our King, here is our love,
Here is our God, who's come to bring us back to Him.
He is the One, He is Jesus, Jesus.
(Second time)
And He is our King, He is our love,
He is our God, who's come to bring us back to Him.
He is the One, He is Jesus, Jesus.

And what was said to the rose to make it unfold
Was said to me here in my chest,
So be quiet now
And rest.

Jesus, our Majesty, finally.
Majesty, finally, You.

1779

Keith & Kristyn Getty & Stuart Townend

FULLNESS OF GRACE in man's human frailty,
This is the wonder of Jesus.
Laying aside His power and glory,
Humbly He entered our world.
Chose the path of meanest worth:
Scandal of a virgin birth.
Born in a stable, cold and rejected:
Here lies the hope of the world.

Fullness of grace, the love of the Father
Shown in the face of Jesus.
Stooping to bear the weight of humanity,
Walking the Calvary road.
Christ the holy Innocent
Took our sin and punishment.
Fullness of God, despised and rejected:
Crushed for the sins of the world.

Fullness of hope in Christ we had longed for,
Promise of God in Jesus.
Through His obedience we are forgiven,
Opening the floodgates of heaven.
All our hopes and dreams we bring
Gladly as an offering.
Fullness of life and joy unspeakable:
God's gift in love to the world.

1780

Geraldine Latty & busbee

GENTLE FATHER, faithful Friend,
God who whispers through the storm;
In every heartbeat, every breath,
I am never on my own.

You alone are my safety,
You alone my hiding place.
Solid ground, open heaven,
Here I'm found within Your grace.

When the questions hide Your face,
When the anxious thoughts arise,
God of heaven, God of peace,
Draw my focus to Your eyes.

There is nothing like Your voice to me
When I hear Your words of hope.
Grace awakened, I am free to be fully loved,
Simply Yours.

Simply Yours, fully loved.
Simply Yours, fully loved.
Simply Yours.

1781

Tim Hughes

GIVER OF LIFE, You never change;
All that is perfect comes from You,
Your wonders never cease.
Not even life, not even death,
Nor any power in heaven or earth
Could separate us from Your love.

For You are good,
And Your mercies last a lifetime.
You are good, always, always.
Every day, Your love is never ending,
For You are good, always, always.

Freely You give, new every day;
Your mercies will never fail,
So great is Your faithfulness.
Your love is kind, Your love is pure,
Your love will always persevere,
For every blessing comes from You.

You delight to pour Your goodness down.
You delight to pour Your goodness down.

1782

Johnny Parks

GLORIOUS, *glorious, glorious is the Lord.*

You shake the deserts with Your voice,
You thunder over the waters.
Let all in the temple rise up and cry:
'Glory, glory, glory!'

Above the flood sits Your throne
From which Your power flows.
You make Your people strong to sing:
'Glory, glory, glory!'

1783

Andy Bromley

GLORIOUS KING,
Seated in the highest place,
Given the Name above all names,
Glorious King.
Glorious King,
Worthy of the highest praise,
Giver of eternal days,
Glorious King, glorious King.

Glorious King,
All the earth declares Your praise,
Speaks the glories of Your name,
Glorious King.
Glorious King,
All creation joins in song,
Lifting up our voice as one,
Glorious King, glorious King.

We come and bow,
We come and bow.
We come and bow
Before our King,
Our glorious King.
(Repeat)

Glorious King,
All the nations bow in awe,
Every king and priest will fall
To their knees.
Glorious King,
On that day Your truth will reign,
We'll sing the glories of Your name,
Glorious King, glorious King.

1784

Keith & Kristyn Getty & Ian Hannah

GLORIOUS LIGHT, see the dawn of salvation;
Angels in white fill the skies with their wondrous song,
Awakening earth with news of His birth:
Join the hymn of the highest heavens.

Long has the world fought the song of the angels;
Heavenly music is drowned by a warring world.
Yet hope burns a light that shatters the night:
Turn your heart to the call of glory.

Glory to God in the highest!
Peace to men on earth.
Come and adore Him with wonder;
Christ, Lord of heaven and earth.

There is a day all creation has longed for,
When all of time has been spent and the Lord returns.
His song we'll repeat as heaven completes
Promised peace that will fill the nations.

1785

Doug Horley

GLORY AND HONOUR TO YOU WE BRING;
Beautiful Saviour, Your praise we sing.
Heaven bows down and worships Your name;
God of creation, we praise.
(Repeat)
God of creation, we praise.

And so to You, we'll give You praise,
We'll give You glory, to You always.
(Repeat)

(We will) honour the King, honour the King,
We will honour the King of kings.
We will honour the King, honour the King,
We will honour the King of kings.
(Repeat)

1786

Gary Clarke & Peter Wilson

GLORY, GLORY ALL AROUND,
As the universe resounds
And we proclaim that He is Lord.
Eternity echoes the song,
Creation joining in as one
And we proclaim that He is Lord.

Heavens cry,
My heart sings,
Jesus is
Lord of all heaven and earth,
Jesus is.

Glorious, the greatest of all,
Jesus is, Jesus is.
Evermore the King above all,
Jesus is, Jesus is.

1787

Lara Martin & Mark Stevens (Abundant Life
Ministries, Bradford, England)

GLORY TO HIM WHO HAS SAVED US
And freed us from sin by His blood.
Jesus, the radiance of God,
The glory of the Father in us.

We crown You now
With worship and honour,
King of kings, Lord of lords,
There's no other.
Holy, holy God Almighty,
Jesus Lord of all.

You are high and lifted up,
High and lifted up,
High and lifted up,
Son of God.

1788

Joel Houston

GOD ABOVE ALL THE WORLD in motion,
God above all my hopes and fears.
And I don't care what the world throws at me now,
It's gonna be all right.

Hear the sound of the generations,
Making loud their freedom song.
All in all that the world would know Your name.
It's gonna be all right.

'Cause I know my God saved the day.
And I know His word never fails.
And I know my God made a way for me.
Salvation is here.

Salvation is here.
Salvation is here and He lives in me.
Salvation is here.
Salvation that died just to set me free.

Salvation is here.
Salvation is here and He lives in me.
Salvation is here.
'Cause You are alive and You live in me.
(Repeat)

1789 Vicky Beeching & Ed Cash

GOD CAME DOWN and gave His life for me,
Amen, amen.
Through flesh and blood He fought for victory,
Amen, amen.
Crucified, brought back to life,
Amen, amen.
Seated at the Father's hand again,
Amen, amen.

Great is the glory of the Lord Almighty;
Great is the glory of the Lord.
I will sing with all my heart unto the Lord Almighty:
Great is Your glory, Lord.

Crimson covered over sinless hands,
Amen, amen.
But nails could never hold the Son of man,
Amen, amen.
Now the Father's love flows down on us,
Amen, amen.
Hallelujah, He will come again,
Amen, amen.

You are the One who was,
You are the One who is,
You are the One who is to come.
(Repeat)

1790

Tim Hughes

GOD IN MY LIVING,
There in my breathing,
God in my waking,
God in my sleeping.
God in my resting,
There in my working,
God in my thinking,
God in my speaking.

Be my everything. *(x4)*

God in my hoping,
There in my dreaming,
God in my watching,
God in my waiting.
God in my laughing,
There in my weeping,
God in my hurting,
God in my healing.

Christ in me, Christ in me,
Christ in me, the hope of glory,
You are everything.
Christ in me, Christ in me,
Christ in me, the hope of glory,
Be my everything.

You are everything…

Jesus, everything…

1791

busbee

GOD OF ALL THE EARTH,
Perfect Son of man,
Love that never turns,
Come and heal our land.
Lord, we need You to move
In our midst as we sing.

Hallelujah, the Lord is King.
All our praises to You we bring.
Humbly ruling with power,
Yet by grace You redeem.
Hallelujah, the Lord is King.

Like a helpless lamb
That has gone astray,
We have chased our plans.
Lord, please change our ways,
So that everyone knows
It's for You that we sing.

Lord, who gives each day,
Give us eyes to see,
That Your perfect way
May direct our feet.
Lord, we long for the world
To join in as we sing.

1792

Keith Getty & Jonathan Rea

GOD OF GRACE, amazing wonder,
Irresistible and free.
Oh, the miracle of mercy;
Jesus reaches down to me.

God of grace, I stand in wonder
As my God restores my soul:
His own blood has paid my ransom;
Awesome cost to make me whole.

God of grace, who loved and knew me
Long before the world began;
Sent my Saviour down from heaven:
Perfect God and perfect man.
God of grace, I trust in Jesus,
I'm accepted as His own.
Every day new grace sustains me
As I lean on Him alone.

God of grace, I stand astounded,
Cleansed, forgiven and secure.
All my fears are now confounded
And my hope is ever sure.
God of grace, now crowned in glory,
Where one day I'll see Your face;
And forever I'll adore You
In Your everlasting grace.

1793

Vicky Beeching, Ed Cash & Kendall Combes

GOD OF HEAVEN, You descended
For all of our sin and shame.
Hands so holy offer healing
For every scar and stain.
And we bow down, we bow down.

Hallelujah, what a Saviour;
We worship and adore.
Hallelujah, what a Saviour;
We glorify the giver of life,
The light of the world.

Holy King of angel armies,
Hanging between two thieves.
Holy feet that walk the heavens
Nailed upon a tree.
And we bow down, we bow down.

We bow down,
(Falling down before Your throne.)
We bow down,
(We glorify You alone.)
We bow down,
(Falling down before Your throne.)
We bow down,
(Glorify You alone.)
(Repeat)

1794

GOD OF JUSTICE, Saviour to all,
Came to rescue the weak and the poor;
Chose to serve and not be served.
Jesus, You have called us.
Freely we've received,
Now freely we will give.

We must go,
Live to feed the hungry,
Stand beside the broken.
We must go.
Stepping forward
Keep us from just singing,
Move us into action,
We must go.

To act justly every day,
Loving mercy in every way,
Walking humbly before You, God.

You have shown us what You require.
Freely we've received,
Now freely we will give.

Fill us up and send us out.
Fill us up and send us out.
Fill us up and send us out, Lord.
(Repeat)

1795

busbee, Gabe Watkins & Malcolm du Plessis

GOD OF OLD, God of the future,
God of all life and all space and all time,
Kindly You've placed Your hand on this tribe;
We're marked by Your blood and Your name.

King of kings, King of the kingdom,
King of all honour and glory and power,
Humbly You followed God's will to the cross
And now rule through vessels of clay.

Lead us on in this holy adventure,
Fill every heart with courage and grace.
May our lives shine so that others are drawn
To the brightness of Your flame.

Lord of lords, Lord of the nations,
Lord over demons, dominions and powers,
You rule supreme over heaven and earth,
You hold our respect and our praise.

Though seasons will change
And visions are tested,
Hindered by obstacles, failure and pain,
You cleanse this house
And purge us with fire;
What cannot be shaken forever remains.

1796

Kate Simmonds & Mark Edwards

GOD SO LOVED THE WORLD
That He gave His only Son,
That all who call on Him shall not die,
But forever more shall live.

Thank You for saving me,
Thank You for changing me.
Lord, You're amazing
And I'm falling at Your feet.
All that You've given me,
Mercy and grace so free,
And for eternity my song of praise shall be:
Your love has come to me.

Jesus on the cross,
By Your blood You made a way
That we can come to God,
To belong and live in this amazing grace.

I recall my life before
You came and changed everything.
Now I know I'm not the same;
This life I've gained makes me brand new.

1797

Godfrey Birtill

GOD SO LOVED THIS WHOLE WORLD
That He gave His only Son,
And if we will cleave to Him
We'll not perish;
But we'll have eternal life
And we'll never be condemned,
For God's promises are Yes and Amen!

Yeah, yeah, yeah! Yeah, yeah, yeah!
Yeah, yeah, yeah! Yeah, yeah, yeah!
Yeah, yeah, yeah!
Yeah, yeah, yeah and Amen!

Though we walk through dark days,
Where the earth and heavens shake,
Through the valley of despair
He is with us;
Never giving up on us,
Faithful and forever friend,
For God's promises are Yes and Amen!

Through the cross we are saved,
In the blood we put our faith,
For there is no other way
Into heaven.
Jesus conquered death and hell,
Promised to return again,
And God's promises are Yes and Amen!

1798

Chris Bowater

GOD, THE LORD,
Creator of heaven and earth,
Gives breath, gives life to the people.
God the Lord,
Who calls you in righteousness,
Will hold you and watch over you,
To make you as light to the nations.

To open blind eyes,
To set prisoners free,
Proclaiming liberty;
Healing the wounds
Of all the oppressed,
And be good news.

The Spirit of the Lord is on me, in me,
Filling me, thrilling me now;
Appointing me, anointing me...

1799 Don Moen

GOD WILL MAKE A WAY
Where there seems to be no way.
He works in ways we cannot see,
He will make a way for me.
He will be my guide,
Hold me closely to His side;
With love and strength
For each new day,
He will make a way,
He will make a way.

By a roadway in the wilderness
He'll lead me,
And rivers in the desert will I see.
Heaven and earth will fade,
But His word will still remain;
He will do something new today.

1800 Rex Allchurch

GOD, YOU ARE FULL OF GRACE AND MERCY,
And I'm standing in the light
Of all You've done for me.
God, You are giving me compassion,
And You teach me what it is to love the lost.

To love the lost with all my heart,
Pick up my cross and follow You.

God, please teach me how to weep
As You weep for all the broken-hearted,
And make me effective in my gifting,
That I can see Your glory falling here.

1801

Kate & Miles Simmonds

GOD, YOU ARE MY GOD,
Earnestly I come.
In a dry and weary land
I thirst for You.
Lover of my soul,
You meet my deepest need;
You are more than all the world can offer me.

For I have seen Your power
And I have seen Your glory,
And who can compare with You?
Who can compare?
And I love You, Lord,
You're my all in all;
I am satisfied in You,
I am satisfied in You.

And in Your name I lift my hands,
So hungry to receive.
I want more of You,
I want more of You.
(Repeat)

1802

Johnny Parks

GOD, YOU ARE MY GOD,
There's no one else like You;
You gladly gave Your blood

To bring me back to You.
I will sing Your praise,
I will lift Your name,
I'll gladly give You all
To see Your kingdom reign.

And I won't be ashamed
When I lift up Your name
To let all the world see
You are the King.
(Repeat)

We give You glory,
Glory to You.
We give You glory,
Glory to You.

Death is overcome,
Forgiven is my sin;
Heaven is my home,
You welcome me in.
I can't wait to hear
The saints join in one song
As we praise the living Son,
Who's given us His all.

1803 Mark Tedder & Gary Sadler

GOD, YOU ARE MY GOD
When darkness falls and my world is shaken.
God, You are my God
When I can't see You at all.
God, You are my God
When I fall and I am broken.
I will choose to trust in You.
Forever I believe . . .

(That) You are with me,
You never leave me,
Your love endures forever.
(Repeat)
God, You are my God.

God, You are my God
When my heart is cold and weak from sin.
God, You are my God
When I can't hear You at all.
God, You are my God,
You pick me up and call me friend.
I will choose to worship You.
Forever I believe . . .

Hallelujah. *(x3)*
Forever I believe . . .

1804

Chris Tomlin, Ed Cash & Jesse Reeves

GOD, YOU HAVE DONE GREAT THINGS.
God, You give grace to the weak,
And bless the broken-hearted
With a song of praise to sing.
You reached down and lifted us up,
You came running, looking for us.
And now there's nothing
And no one beyond Your love.

You're the overflow,
You're the fountain of my heart,
So let Your mercy rain,
Let Your mercy rain on us.
You're the faithful One
When the world's falling apart.
So let Your mercy rain,
Let Your mercy rain on us.

How deep, how wide,
How long, how high
Is Your love, is Your love.
(Repeat)
O God.

1805

Chris Tomlin, Jesse Reeves,
Cary Pierce & Jon Able

GREAT ARE YOU, LORD, mighty in strength;
You are faithful and You will ever be.
We will praise You all of our days;
It's for Your glory we offer everything.

Raise your hands, all you nations,
Shout to God, all creation:
How awesome is the Lord most high.

(Second time)
We will praise You together
For now and for ever;
How awesome is the Lord most high.

Where You send us, God, we will go;
You're the answer we want the world to know.
We will trust You when You call our name;
Where You lead us, we'll follow all the way.

Hallelujah, hallelujah.
How awesome is the Lord most high.
(Repeat)

Hallelujah, hallelujah.
(Repeat)

1806

Chris Bowater

GREATER GRACE, DEEPER MERCY,
Wider love, higher ways.
Perfect peace, complete forgiveness,
It's all found in You,
It's all found in You.

More than hope, full assurance,
Joy that more than satisfies.
Comfort, strength, power and healing,
It's all found in You,
It's all found in You.

It's all found in You, Jesus,
It's all found in You;
All I desire and all I require,
It's all found in You.

Mercy triumphs over justice;
Judgement is good, mercy is best.
Where sin abounds
Grace is more abounding,
It's all found in You.

1807

Lex Buckley & Tim Hughes

GREATER THAN ANY OTHER NAME,
You are the Lord;
Worthy to be adored and praised
Forever more.

So I gaze upon Your beauty,
As You reveal Your glory
In this place.
I fall to my knees, I fall to my knees.

Surrounded by Your splendour,
This heart is filled with wonder,
Love and praise.
I fall to my knees, I fall to my knees.

Humbly I come to seek Your face,
Longing for more.
With just a glimpse of You I'm changed,
Glorious God.

And I'll never be the same;
Forever I am changed.
I'll never be the same;
Jesus, I am changed.
I'll never be the same.

1808

Carey Luce & Geraldine Latty

(Men)
GREAT GOD, *hear the song that we sing.*
Great God, You're the welcoming King.

(Women)
Coming to worship, coming to praise You,
Coming to say that You are God.
(Repeat)

You have called us to Your table,
Young and old together here.
What a family You make us,
As You call us we draw near.

Thank You for the gifts You give us,
Thank You for Your presence here.
By the Spirit working in us
We will worship without fear.

May our story be Your story,
May our lives be wholly Yours,
So that others come to worship
Jesus Christ the Lord of all.

1809

Andy Bromley

GREAT GOD of wonders,
Great God in power,
The heavens are declaring
The glories of Your name,
The glories of Your name.

Great God of Zion,
Great God in beauty,
The nations are gathering
To worship at Your feet,
To worship at Your feet.

From the rising to the setting sun,
Your name will be praised.
God above all gods,
King above all kings,
Lord of heaven and earth.
We give You praise, praise, praise.
We give You praise, praise, praise.

You are the great God above all gods,
You are the great King above all kings,
You are the great Lord of heaven and earth.
We give You praise.
(Repeat)
We give You praise, praise, praise.
We give You praise, praise, praise.

1810

Reuben Morgan

GREAT IS THE LORD GOD ALMIGHTY,
Great is the Lord on high.
The train of His robe fills the temple,
And we cry out highest praise.

Glory to the risen King,
Glory to the Son, glorious Son.

Lift up your heads, open the doors,
Let the King of glory come in
And forever be our God.

Holy is the Lord God Almighty,
Holy is the Lord on high.
Let all the earth bow before You,
And crown You Lord of all.

1811

Chris Tomlin

GREAT IS YOUR FAITHFULNESS,
Great is Your faithfulness.
You never change,
You never fail, O God.

True are Your promises,
True are Your promises.
You never change,
You never fail, O God.

So we raise up holy hands
To praise the holy One,
Who was, and is, and is to come.

Yeah, we raise up holy hands
To praise the holy One,
Who was, and is, and is to come.

Wide is Your love and grace,
Wide is Your love and grace.
You never change,
You never fail, O God.

You were, You are, You will always be.
You were, You are, You will always be.

1812

Matt Maher add. lyrics Chris Tomlin

GREAT IS YOUR FAITHFULNESS, O God;
You wrestle with the restless heart.
You lead us by still waters into mercy,
And nothing can keep us apart.

So, remember Your people,
Remember Your children,
Remember Your promise, O God.

Your grace is enough,
Your grace is enough,
Your grace is enough for me.

Great is Your love and justice, God of Jacob;
You use the weak to lead the strong.
You lead us in the song of Your salvation,
And all Your people sing along.

Your grace is enough,
Heaven reaching down to us.
Your grace is enough for me.
God, I see Your grace is enough;
I'm covered in Your love.
Your grace is enough for me, for me.

1813 Keith Getty & Margaret Becker

HAIL TO THE GLADDENING LIGHT of pure glory,
We come rejoicing in You.
Hail to the worthiest Holy of holies,
Let Your glory be ever known.

Now in the company of all heaven's angels,
We join creation in song
To You who have covered the mountains with water;
Let Your glory be ever known.

With our mouths we bless You,
With our lives confess You:
Christ, hallowed on high,
Hosanna evermore.

Come, for Your Spirit has filled us with longing
That only You satisfy.
Great are You, Lord, and Your wonders are countless;
Let Your glory be ever known.

Joy of the morning and life everlasting,
Let Your love fill us afresh.
For all we can give You is what You have given;
Let Your glory be ever known.

1814 Noel Robinson & Donna Akodu

HALLELUJAH, HALLELUJAH, hallelujah.
I adore You, precious Saviour, hallelujah.

Hallelujah, hallelujah is the song we sing.
With our voices giving praises
As we enter in.

You delight, Lord, in our praises;
Come inhabit now.
We adore You, bow before You,
Praise before Your throne.

High and exalted, risen Saviour,
The redeeming Son.
Casting down our treasure
To be Your pleasure,
We come to worship now.

Glory to the King,
Glory to the King,
Glory to the King most high.

1815

David Gate

HANDS ON THE CROSS
That had once held the earth,
Thorns on the brow
Where once was heaven's crown:
Surrendered and humbled to death,
Emptied and suffering with every breath.

The Son, the Man,
The Christ, the Lamb,
The maker of all things,
Jesus.

Raised from the tomb
And now sits on His throne;
Soon to return
And to welcome us home:
In splendour and wonder and might,
With colour and fire and blinding light.

1816

Lex Buckley

HAVE MERCY ON ME, O God of love;
I recognise my sin.
This heart is heavy with guilt and shame,
So in brokenness I sing.

Wash me and I will be whiter than the snow,
Cleanse me and I will be clean.
Saviour, forgive me for all that I have done,
For I long to run into Your arms.

Lord, help me to live this life with You,
To follow all Your ways.
I'm longing to have a heart that's pure,
To be more like You each day.

Lord, fill this heart with joy again;
Let it overflow with Your praise.
Fill this heart with joy again;
Let it overflow with Your praise.

1817

Doug Horley

HAVE WE MADE OUR GOD TOO SMALL, *too small?*
Have we made our God too small?
He made the heavens and earth
And He reigns on high,
Yet He's got the time for you and I.

See the glory of God light up the sky
As the clouds proclaim He reigns on high.
See the huge expanse of the oceans wide
And a billion stars that grace the sky.

I am awed by the power,
Awed by the marks of God all around me.
Yet I'm humbled every day
By my unbelieving ways;
I really, really want it to change.

1818

Andy Bromley & Chris Bowater

HEALING GRACE is flowing,
Wells of hope are springing up,
Cleansing streams of kindness
Touching me,
Transforming me.

I am made whole,
I am made whole;
In Jesus, my Lord,
I am made whole.
(Repeat)

1819

Keith & Kristyn Getty & Stuart Townend

HEAR THE CALL OF THE KINGDOM,
Lift your eyes to the King.
Let His song rise within you
As a fragrant offering
Of how God, rich in mercy,
Came in Christ to redeem
All who trust in His unfailing grace.

Hear the call of the kingdom
To be children of light,
With the mercy of heaven,
The humility of Christ.
Walking justly before Him,

Loving all that is right,
That the life of Christ may shine through us.

King of heaven, we will answer the call;
We will follow, bringing hope to the world,
Filled with passion, filled with power to proclaim
Salvation in Jesus' name.

Hear the call of the kingdom
To reach out to the lost
With the Father's compassion,
In the wonder of the cross,
Bringing peace and forgiveness
And a hope yet to come;
Let the nations put their trust in Him.

1820 Chris Tomlin, Ed Cash & Jesse Reeves

HEAR THE HOLY ROAR of God resound,
Watch the waters part before us now.
Come and see what He has done for us,
Tell the world of His great love.

Our God is a God who saves.
Our God is a God who saves.

Let God arise,
Let God arise.
Our God reigns now and forever,
He reigns now and forever.

His enemies will run for sure,
The church will stand, she will endure.
He holds the keys of life, our Lord,
Death has no sting, no final word.

1821 Graham Kendrick

HEAR US NOW, O LOVING GOD,
We pray for this our world;
Oh, hear the words of our confession.
We have bowed to other gods
And crowded out Your voice,
Allowed injustice and oppression.
When will we return to You?
Father, Father,
Turn us back to loving You.

Only You deserve the praise,
Only You deserve the song.
O Lord, it all belongs to You.
Only You deserve the love,
Only You deserve the thanks.
O Lord, it all belongs to You.

For the children of this land
We lift to You our hands,
And ask You, Father, please have mercy.
For innocence betrayed,
Forgive us, Lord, we pray,
And once again pour out Your Spirit.
When will we return to You?
Father, Father,
Turn us back to loving You.

For the earth in deep distress,
Our greed, our selfishness,
Oh, hear the words of our confession.
Oh, teach us how to share,
Restore, renew, repair,
And welcome in Your new creation.
When will we return to You?
Father, Father,
Turn us back to loving You.

1822

Matt Redman, Josiah Bell & Robin Marvin

HEAR YOUR PEOPLE SAYING YES,
Hear Your people saying yes to You.
Yes to anything You ask,
Yes to anything we're called to do.

Hear Your people say amen,
Hear Your people say amen to You.
Let Your kingdom come on earth,
Let it be just like we prayed to You.

Yes and amen
To everything that's in Your heart.
Yes and amen
To everything that You have planned.
We live to see Your will be done,
And see Your perfect kingdom
Come on earth, on the earth.
Yes and amen,
We're taking up our cross for You.
Give us the strength
To take these dreams and follow through.
We live to see Your will be done,
And see Your perfect kingdom
Come on earth, on the earth.

All the promises are yes,
All the promises are yes in You.
Every good and perfect gift,
Every blessing that we have was You.

1823

Noel Richards & Kees Kraayenoord

HEAVEN'S KING,
Who created everything,
Is there something I could bring
To You?
A thousand songs –
Could they ever be enough
To thank You for Your Father's love
For me?

Here I am.
Here I am.

I bring my heart, my hands, my feet,
To share Your love with those in need.
Let it be my song of love for You.
Use my voice to tell Your story.
Use my arms to hold the lonely.
Let that be my song of love for You.

Heaven's King,
Who created everything,
Is there something I could bring
To You?
Saviour,
You desire truth within
A broken and a willing heart
For You.

1824 Brian Doerksen & Paul Baloche

HE IS HERE, *He is near us,*
In our hearts, in our lives, in our midst.
He is here, He is near us,
Calling us to trust in Him.
(Repeat)

Cast your every care
On the One who gave you life,
Lay your burdens down at His feet.
Open up your hearts to the living Word of God;
He is love, He is love.

He is here, He is near us,
Calling us to trust in Him,
Calling us to trust in Him.

1825 Rex Allchurch

HELP ME TO BE HOLY,
Teach me what it is;
Living out this daily,
Offering myself.
Help me to be humble,
Teach me what it is;
Looking to You daily,
Offering to You.

I long to be with You, my precious;
I want to sing to You my praises.
I want to honour You
With every part of my life.

Guide me in my lifestyle,
Teach me how to live;
Follow Your example,
Offering myself.
Guide me in my calling,
Teach me how to live;
Lost in adoration,
Offering to You.

1826

Paul Baloche & Brenton Brown

HERE AND NOW, *here in this moment,*
Here and now I turn to You.
All that my searching heart has longed for
Can be found,
'Cause You're in this moment,
Here and now.

What majesty, what mystery,
The God of all eternity
Stepped into time and gave His life for me.
Your hand is seen in galaxies,
Yet Your Spirit dwells in me;
So vast and yet You're still within our reach.

There is nowhere You can't be found;
Nothing on earth could ever keep Your presence out.

1827

Martin Smith & Stuart Garrard

HERE I AM,
Humbled by Your majesty,
Covered by Your grace so free.
Here I am,
Knowing I'm a sinful man,
Covered by the blood of the Lamb.

Now I've found
The greatest love of all is mine,
Since You laid down Your life,
The greatest sacrifice.

Majesty, majesty.
Your grace has found me just as I am,
Empty-handed but alive in Your hands.
Majesty, majesty.
Forever I am changed by Your love
In the presence of Your majesty.

Here I am,
Humbled by the love that You give,
Forgiven so that I can forgive.
Here I stand,
Knowing that I'm Your desire,
Sanctified by glory and fire.

1828

Matt Redman

HERE I AM, I'M A SOUL SET FREE,
Caught up in this mystery.
Jesus, there is a hope I breathe,
For You are in me, You are in me.
Here I am with my chains undone,
Caught up in Your victory.
Singing songs of a higher love,
For You are with me, You are with me,
And we are ever praising You.

You brought a blessing,
And the blessing was You, yeah, yeah.
There was a treasure,
And the treasure was You, yeah, yeah.
Lord, we had nothing, now we have all things,

We were the lost, but found the truth.
You brought a blessing,
And the blessing was You.

(Last chorus)
Jesus, the blessing is You,
Jesus, the blessing is You,
Oh, Jesus, the blessing is You.

As I walk through the valley low,
I will build a place of hope.
Going on from strength to strength,
For You are in me, You are in me.
Nothing good do You withhold
From the one who walks in Your way.
I'd give it all for just one day
That You are with me, You are with me.
Yes, we are ever praising You.

Hearts can find no rest until they find You.
You made us for Yourself and we will praise You.
(Repeat)
We will praise You.

1829

Matt Weedall

HERE I AM, MY GOD,
I've come to seek Your face;
I long to know You more in my life.
So here I am, my Lord,
I want to meet with You;
I long to know Your glory in this place.

My heart yearns for You.
My soul thirsts for You.

'Cause You're my rock,
You're my light,
You're my hope,
You're my song in the night.
You're the air that I breathe;
You're the food my soul wants,
My soul needs.

1830

Andy Bromley, John Hartley & Gary Sadler

HERE I AM, STANDING AMAZED,
Your wonders before me
Displaying Your glory.
The One by whom all things were made;
What can define You?
No words can describe You.
We will see You,
And we will see You.

Glorious Majesty,
Ruler of history,
You gave Your life for me,
I will praise You.
Glorious Majesty,
Beauty that captures me,
Your love has set me free.
I will praise You.

Like angels who look at Your face,
Gaze at Your glory,
Cry 'Holy holy',
Adoring the King of all days,
Fall down before You,
Forever to love You.
We will see You,
Yes, we will see You.

1831

Nick Herbert & David Gate

HERE IN THE SHADOW OF YOUR HOLINESS,
Where I can barely speak Your praise,
More than a moment in Your sanctuary,
This is the promise of Your grace,
This is the promise of Your grace:
Here I'll stay.

Thousands of angels standing at Your side,
Millions of voices sing Your praise.
So humbled, Lord, that You would welcome me;
This is the promise of Your grace,
This is the promise of Your grace:
Here I'll stay.

How can I not adore You?
How can I not adore You
For the promise of Your grace?

1832

Michael Sandeman

HERE I STAND, *covered by grace,*
Under the blood that was shed for me.
Here I kneel before the King upon His throne.
Here I bow to worship the Lord,
Enjoying His favour on my life today,
Knowing that we'll never be apart.

I'm a child of God,
Created for my maker's pleasure,
Chosen to enjoy Him forever,
Granted dignity by what He says about me.
Made in His image,
Precious in the eyes of my Father,
Purchased by the death of my Saviour,
I have been given life to the full.

In a spacious place,
I'm basking in the warmth of the sunshine;
The Holy Spirit's tender presence
Brings such joy to me and such liberty.
I'm standing firm,
Holding fast to all He's spoken,
No promise He's made will be broken;
I live by faith in Jesus Christ.

And I won't believe all the lies that I hear,
When low self-esteem whispers into my ear
That I'm worthless and poor,
That I'm lost and alone;
At moments like that I must look to the throne.

1833

Shaun Griffiths

HERE I STAND IN AWE OF YOU;
Though others don't understand,
I know You are the truth.
Your goodness and Your mercy,
Your never-failing love,
Lead me to draw close to You.

Here I am worshipping You;
With all my heart I lift my love to You.
Your faithfulness and goodness,
Your all-consuming love,
Lead me to draw close to You.

You are holy, the heavens shout Your name.
You are holy, forever You're the same.
You are holy, I stand amazed.
No one can compare to You.
That's why I love You like I do.

I love You, God. I wanna say that *(x3)*
I love You, God.

1834

Kelley Warren, Robert Critchley & Darlene Dunn

HERE I STAND IN YOUR PRESENCE,
Calling out to You:
More of You and less of me,
Cleanse my heart, set me free.
I want to look into Your eyes,
Know the secrets of Your heart,
But most of all this is my cry:
I want to be loved by You.

My desire is to see Your face.
My desire is to feel Your embrace.
My desire is to know without a doubt
That You will never let me go;
This is the desire of my heart.

Your love wraps around my heart
Like the wings of an angel;
Makes me feel secure in my Father's arms.

1835

Jarrod Cooper & Carol Owen

HE'S ALIVE,
Death and hell have been defeated.
He's alive,
And the grave has been denied.
He's alive,
Sin no longer has dominion,
For the grave is empty –
Jesus is alive.

There is healing, there's deliverance,
There is power and forgiveness;
He has broken every chain

For those in darkness,
Those in shame:
For the grave is empty –
Jesus is alive.

There is freedom, there is victory,
There is comfort, there is joy;
He has opened prison doors,
Returned to dancing those who mourn:
For the grave is empty –
Jesus is alive.

1836

Johnny Parks & Phil Mawhinney

HE'S BEYOND CONTROL,
Bigger than we know,
Untied and untamed,
Holy is His name.

He rages like the storms,
Burns like the sun,
Stirs like the deep,
Nations at His feet.

Heaven overflows
With the sound of praise;
Nothing can contain
This almighty sound.

Poets can't explain,
History can't retain,
Science can't define
The wonders of Your name.

Turn it up...
This almighty sound.

1837

HIDE ME NOW under Your wings.
Cover me within Your mighty hand.

When the oceans rise and thunders roar,
I will soar with You above the storm.
Father, You are King over the flood;
I will be still and know You are God.

Find rest, my soul, in Christ alone.
Know His power in quietness and trust.

1838

HIS WOUNDS, MY HEALING;
His blood, my peace.
His pain, my freedom;
His death, my life.
His death, my life,
His death, my life.

1839

HOLY CHILD, who chose the hearts of men
To be His favoured home;
Leaving heaven's gates for Bethlehem,
God came to call His own.
Now to us the highest King is born;
Behold the royal Son.
Glory kneels to bind up all that's torn:
The promised One has come.

Joy and pain as man He knew on earth,
No place to lay His head.
As a servant He embraced this world
And on a cross He bled.
Having borne the deepest grief of man
He rose to heaven's throne;
Now I'm sheltered in the Father's hand
Until He calls me home.

May the gift of God amaze us still,
The triumph of all time.
As His child I kneel to heaven's will
To make His purpose mine.
Though this road be scarred with trial and pain,
It's paved with lavish grace.
Knowing Him will be my greatest gain,
His throne my resting place.

1840

Nathan Fellingham & Robin Parry

HOLY FATHER, we thank You
For giving us Your Son,
Who gave His life as a ransom,
A covenant of blood.
Now we remember Your mercy
In doing this for us,
And Jesus, by the Spirit,
We know You're here with us.

With joy we will partake in
The benefits You've given.
Through dying on the cross
You have made peace with us.

We will draw near to You, Father,
Hearing the call of the Spirit.
The work of the Son is completed,

A new way of life has now begun.
A people believing Your promise,
Filled with the power of the Spirit,
And we look forward to that day
When Jesus returns to take us home,
Forever invited to share
With the Godhead, three in one.

1841

Kate & Miles Simmonds

HOLY GOD,
Generations know Your promises,
Your covenant of love.
Lord of all,
Every promise made
You remain faithful to fulfil.
For Your ways are holy
And Your name is worthy;
All honour and glory belong to You.

(For) You are faithful, mighty, glorious,
Awesome and victorious,
Beautiful and wonderful, Lord.
Now our hearts are resolute;
Our confidence is all in You,
Everything is possible, O Lord, my Lord.

When troubles come, when life overwhelms,
You are Lord, You are in control.
I trust in You, for in my darkest day
You remain worthy of my praise!
For Your ways are higher,
And Your arm is stronger,
And Your rest is sweeter than any other.

1842

Graeme Clark

HOLY GOD, You reign over all things;
You alone shall have my praise.
Faithful Friend, You never leave me,
My soul rejoices at Your name.

Glorious King, my praises rise to You:
A fire burns within my heart.
All my days my praise will rise to You,
Singing, 'Jesus, I love Your name.
Jesus, I love Your name.'

By Your blood You've given me freedom;
I give You back the life I owe.
My life, a sacrifice before You now,
'Cause You deserve the best from me.

Jesus, yes I love Your name,
For the mighty things You've done for me,
For the death upon the cross that set me free.
(Repeat)

1843

Lou & Nathan Fellingham & busbee

HOLY GROUND,
We are standing on holy ground.
Here before Your throne with open arms
We worship You.
(Repeat)

You are holy,
You are worthy
To receive power, wisdom and strength.

In their thousands
Angels worship,
Giving praise and all glory to You.

Holy One,
In all earth and heaven there is none
To compare with You;
Your glory outshines the sun.
(Repeat)

Heaven and earth will change,
But You remain the Lord of all.
We are standing here on holy ground.

1844 Brian Doerksen

HOLY, HOLY, HOLY GOD.
Holy, holy, holy God.

Creating, commanding,
Transcendent Adonai;
Defending love, destroying sin,
The warrior divine.

Forgiving, redeeming,
From every tribe and tongue;
Arising first, the nail-scarred Lamb,
Salvation's champion.

Romancing, pursuing,
Reclaiming to restore;
Releasing hearts, transforming lives,
The Lion's mighty roar.

1845

Reuben Morgan

HOLY, HOLY, I WILL BOW
Before my Lord and King.
Hallelujah,
You have come to us,
You make all things new.

Emmanuel, Jesus Christ,
You'll never let me go.
My Shepherd King,
You're watching over me,
Emmanuel.

So amazing,
You have named the stars
Of the deepest night.
Still You love me,
You have called my name;
I will follow You.

Holy, holy, God Almighty,
There is none like You.
(Repeat)

1846

Marty Sampson

HOLY ONE, holy One,
All creation bows to worship.
Hallelujah, hallelujah,
Glory in the highest.
I will sing, I will sing His praises forever.

God, He reigns,
God, He reigns;
Holy is the Lord of heaven.
God, He reigns,
God, He reigns forever more.

1847

Mike Sandeman & Nathan Fellingham

HOLY SPIRIT, from before the dawn of time
You have always been the Father's breath divine.
Brooding on the waters,
Bringing forth new life,
Teaching, guiding, shining out Your light,
Making known the mysteries of Christ.
And we long to feel You here.
Holy Spirit, please draw near.

Come, holy fire, burn so free,
Your presence purifying me.
You glorify the risen One.
Sweet Holy Spirit, flow through me;
This glimpse of power, this guarantee,
A foretaste of the age to come.

Holy Spirit, You're our counsellor and friend;
Helper, uniter, You're the One whom Jesus sent.
Make me more like Jesus;
Spirit, have free reign.
Abba Father, Your voice within us cries:
We're loved and precious in our Father's eyes.
As we give ourselves to You,
Holy Spirit, fill this room.

Fill me up each day,
Fill me up each hour.
Fill me with Your love,
Fill me with Your power.
(Repeat)

1848

Geraldine Latty

HOLY SPIRIT, BREATH OF HEAVEN,
Holy Spirit, breathe on us.
Breathe us to a quiet stillness
Where we trust Your love for us.

Holy Spirit, breath of heaven,
Holy Spirit, breathe on us.
Breathe us to a quiet stillness
Where we find Your place for us.

Holy Spirit, breath of heaven,
Holy Spirit, breathe on us.
Breathe us to a quiet stillness
Where we know that You are God.

1849

Miriam Webster

HOLY SPIRIT, HOLY SPIRIT,
Comforter, Counsellor, here.

Holy Spirit, sent from heaven,
The God of all glory is here.

Rise up within me, Living Water,
Spirit of God in me.

You are welcome in this place,
You are welcome in this place.
God of power, love and grace,
Saturate my soul.

Closest Friend, here in Your presence
Is fullness of joy overflowing.

1850

Keith Getty & Stuart Townend

HOLY SPIRIT, LIVING BREATH OF GOD,
Breathe new life into my willing soul.
Bring the presence of the risen Lord
To renew my heart and make me whole.
Cause Your word to come alive in me,
Give me faith for what I cannot see;
Give me passion for Your purity;
Holy Spirit, breathe new life in me.

Holy Spirit, come abide within,
May Your joy be seen in all I do.
Love enough to cover every sin
In each thought and deed and attitude:
Kindness to the greatest and the least,
Gentleness that sows the path of peace.
Turn my strivings into works of grace;
Breath of God, show Christ in all I do.

Holy Spirit, from creation's birth,
Giving life to all that God has made,
Show Your power once again on earth,
Cause Your church to hunger for Your ways.
May the fragrance of our prayers arise;
Lead us on the road of sacrifice,
That in unity the face of Christ
May be clear for all the world to see.

1851

Paul Oakley
Additional lyrics by Kate Simmonds

HOLY SPIRIT, YOU ARE HERE NOW,
And we say that You are Lord.
Holy Spirit, how we love You,
And we bow our hearts in awe.

For Your presence is the presence of the King.
Holy Spirit, come and fill our hearts again,
Come glorify Jesus' name.

In Your mercy there is healing,
And we lay our burdens down.
Have Your way, Lord; as we worship
We are changed by Your mighty power.

Hallelujah, hallelujah,
I am Yours and You are mine.
My beloved, I surrender;
Not my will but Yours be done.

Fall upon us, anoint us with Your power.
Purify us, all-consuming fire;
Come glorify Jesus' name.

1852

Chris Tomlin & J. D. Walt

HOLY, UNCREATED ONE,
Your beauty fills the skies,
But the glory of Your majesty
Is the mercy in Your eyes.

And worthy, uncreated One,
From heaven to earth come down,
You laid aside Your royalty
To wear the sinner's crown.

O great God, be glorified,
Our lives laid down, Yours magnified.
And O great God, be lifted high;
There is none like You.

Jesus, Saviour, God's own Son,
Risen, reigning Lord.
Sustainer of the universe
By the power of Your word.

And when we see Your matchless face,
In speechless awe we'll stand.
And there we'll bow with grateful hearts
Unto the great I Am.

1853

Andy Smith

HOW CAN I BECOME
All that I can be?
How on earth can I
Finally be free?
Though I'm far from home,
How can I return,
Knowing that Your love
Is nothing I can earn?

Forgiven, forgiven, forgiven, forgiven.

My heart is black and cold,
So filthy with my sin.
I know it's only You
That makes me new within.
You quiet me with Your love,
Now I can hear Your song;
You sing it over me
And I know that I belong.

Oh, clothed in majesty,
Yet mindful of me.
Oh, You've come into my heart,
Saviour, Redeemer, You've set me apart.

1854

Paul Oakley & Lex Loizides

HOW CAN I RESIST
This love that draws my heart,
This voice that calls my name?
I'll never be the same again.
How could I deny
This King who took my place,
The One who bore my shame?
I run into these arms of grace.
How could I refuse?
I choose to follow You.

This is for me,
This blood of Christ,
Washing all my stains,
Breaking all my chains.
This is for me,
This death He died,
Taking all my sin,
Giving me a chance to live again.

I choose to follow You;
You gave Your life for me.
I choose to follow You;
Jesus, I believe.

1855

Andy Bromley, John Hartley & Dennis Holt

HOW CAN MY WORDS BEGIN TO SAY
How much Your love has changed my days,
Changed my days?
How perfect peace restored my soul,
You brought me life, made me whole,
You made me whole.

When I think of what You've done,
With all my heart I'll praise the One.
With every breath this song will rise to You.

Because of You, because of You,
Everything I am and everything I owe to You.
Because of You, because of You,
My life will never be the same,
And it's all because of You.

1856

Nigel Briggs, Rich Bull, Matthias Loose & Phil Squires

HOW COULD I NOT BE ON YOUR SIDE
Now You've shown me
What it means to be alive?
What can I give to show You
How much You've changed me,
Now I'll never be the same?

So I will act justly, love mercy,
Walk humbly with my God.
I will act justly, love mercy,
Walk humbly with my God.

Seasons they change, passions they fade,
But one thing's for sure:
You will always remain
King of my heart.
Jesus, You are always with me,
And I'll never be the same.

Nothing can separate us from this love.
Nothing could ever stand in Your way.
Nothing can separate us from our God –
Forever and ever You will reign.

1857

Noel & Tricia Richards

HOW EASY WE FORGET that cross of shame,
Where One who did no wrong
Took all the blame, because of love.

How easy we forget the love You show;
How welcoming You are
To everyone who cries to You.

Break our hearts again.
Break our hearts again.

How weary we become of doing good.
How deaf and blind we are
To those who hurt, who cry for help.

To love as You have loved,
To be a friend.
To comfort those who mourn,
And dry their tears.
To hold the broken-hearted,
Share their pain.

1858

Keith Getty & Margaret Becker

HOW GOOD, HOW PLEASING to God in heaven
When brothers in unity dwell.
How sweet, how fragrant a testament
When brothers in unity dwell.
Like the dew that blesses the highest mount,
Flowing down.
How good to love as Christ has loved,
One in our precious Lord.

How good, how pleasing to God in heaven
When brothers in unity dwell.
How sweet, how fragrant a testament
When brothers in unity dwell.
Let the saints come return to God
With forgiving hearts.
How good to love as Christ has loved,
One in our precious Lord.

How good, how pleasing to God in heaven
When brothers in unity dwell.
How sweet, how fragrant a testament
When brothers in unity dwell.
Till the day heaven's host will join with man
To praise the Lamb.
How good to love as Christ has loved,
One in our precious Lord.

1859

Al Gordon

HOW LONG till we gaze upon Your face,
Gaze upon Your face, gaze upon Your face?
Jesus, we will gaze upon Your face
In the morning light.

How long till You wipe these tears away,
Wipe these tears away, wipe these tears away?
Jesus, You will wipe these tears away
When the morning comes.

Yes, I know You will come.
Yes, I know You've already won.
Yes, I know my Redeemer lives,
My Redeemer lives.

How long till there's justice on the earth,
Justice on the earth, justice on the earth?

Jesus, there'll be justice on the earth
When You come again.

Come, Lord Jesus!
We are desperate for You here.
Come, Lord Jesus!
All creation calling out!
Yeah, yeah, yeah.

How long till we hear the victory roar,
Hear the victory roar, hear the victory roar?
Jesus, we will hear the victory roar
When this race is run.

1860

Tim Hughes & Martin Smith

I AM CHOSEN, I am free,
I am living for eternity,
Free now forever.
You pick me up, turn me around,
You set my feet on solid ground;
Yours now forever.

And nothing's gonna hold me back,
Nothing's gonna hold me back,
Nothing's gonna hold me back.

My chains fell off, my heart was free;
I'm alive to live for You,
I'm alive to live for You.
Amazing love, how can it be?
You gave everything for me,
You gave everything for me,
Everything.

(Last time)
I give everything for You,
I give everything for You,
Everything.

You've washed my sin and shame away,
The slate is clean, a brand new day;
Free now forever.
Now boldly I approach Your throne
To claim this crown through Christ my own,
Yours now forever.

And I'm free to live, free to give,
Free to be, I'm free to love You.
I'm free to live, free to give,
Free to be, I'm free to love You, Lord.

1861

Jim Bailey

I AM FEARFULLY AND WONDERFULLY MADE.
I am fearfully and wonderfully made.
He who put the stars in place
And knows them all by name
Has made me fearfully and wonderfully made.

I am made in the image of God.
I am made in the image of God.
From the top of my head
To the tips of my toes,
My Lord, my name He knows.
I am made in the image of God.

1862

Evan Rogers

I AM FILLED WITH JOY now that I'm free.
Lord, You paid the price for my iniquities.
Your forgiveness I could never earn,
And You have not treated me
As my sins deserve.

I'm giving You ecstatic praise,
For You are good and You are great.
Your love and grace I've understood;
There is no God compared to You.
I'm overwhelmed, I must express
And praise You with exuberance.
The life I lead, the praise I give
Can only be like You: extravagant!

You are worthy of all passionate praise.
We rejoice for we are those who are being saved.
I cannot stay silent or reserved.
I have tasted of Your love,
Now my heart is stirred.

1863

Nathan & Lou Fellingham & busbee

I AM HARD PRESSED on every side,
But I'm not crushed.
I feel pulled to pieces,
But inside I know I'm not.
Feels like the world's caving in,
Find it hard to breathe.
The water is rising –
Won't You come and rescue me?
I'm on my knees.
O God, please come to me.

I fall into Your loving arms,
You wrap me up and I'm secure.
Patiently You whisper to me You have a plan;
To hold on, it won't be long and You understand.
You know my every need;
You won't abandon me.

Sick inside again today,
I'm struggling to pray
And my head is spinning,
'Cause I cannot see the way.
I'm in need of direction,
Everything seems so unclear.
O my God, are You out there,
Or is this falling on deaf ears?
I'm on my knees.
O God, please come to me.

Miracles You will do,
As I come and put my hope in You.
(Repeat)

1864

Dave Bilbrough

I AM NOT ALONE, God is watching over me.
Every step I take, He is watching over me.
He's faithful, so faithful.

God surrounds me with His love,
He is always near;
In my deepest need, through my darkest hour,
He won't ever leave or forsake me.

1865

Paul Oakley

I AM NOT ASHAMED,
I'm not afraid to say,
Jesus, You have made my heart believe.
Your grace alone has saved me.
The truth has set this captive free.
You turned my life around,
Chose me as Your own,
Jesus, You have placed Your life in me.
And I cannot contain such love,
This hope of glory You have placed in me.

Oh, the wonder and the power of the cross,
It's foolishness to those who cannot see.
But every day I wake to find
Your blood goes on forever cleansing me.

Hallelujah! Hallelujah!
Hallelujah! Hallelujah!

1866

Matt Redman & Martin Smith

I AM NOT A STRANGER TO MERCY,
For You found me,
Wrapped Your truth around me.
I am not a stranger to grace;
I have seen it in Your face.
I am not a stranger to kindness;
We're the broken with Your life inside us.
You have brought Your gospel to me,
And I breathe it every day.
How did I become Your miracle?
Now to take Your truth and tell the world.

I'm going to take it to the streets,
I'm going to sing it till we meet.
Heaven is open – come on, all the earth rejoice.
I'm going to take it to the streets,
Wake up the dead heart from its sleep.
Heaven is open – now's the time to raise our voice.

I must tell the world of this mercy,
For You found me,
Wrapped Your truth around me.
I must tell the world of this grace;
I have seen it at Your cross.
I must tell the world of this kindness;
We're the broken with Your life inside us.
You have brought Your gospel to me;
Help me live it every day.
How did we become Your miracles?
Now to take Your truth and tell the world.

1867

Andy Smith

I BELIEVE IN THE POWER OF YOUR BLOOD,
Cleansing me from all my shame.
I am the righteousness of God,
You took all the guilt and blame.

Now I stand complete,
Perfect in Your sight.
Grace has won my heart;
Now I'm walking in the light.

Thank You for the cross,
Thank You for the blood,
Thank You for the gift You've given to us.
Thank You for the tears,
Thank You for the pain,
Thank You that You died and rose again
So I can stand complete in You.

I believe by Your wounds we are healed –
Freedom from a past of pain.
Jesus has broken every curse;
Sickness bows down to Your name.

I believe in the risen Lamb of God,
Seated at the Father's side,
Angels crying 'Holy is the Lord!'
King forever glorified.

1868

Darlene Zschech

I BELIEVE IN YOU,
The joy of my salvation.
I believe in You,
The Saviour of my life.

For without You I can do nothing,
But with You I am strong
To follow in Your truth, Jesus;
I believe in You.

I believe in You,
A fire burns within me.
I believe in You,
My life will bring You praise.

I owe You my life,
I will worship You forever.
I owe You my life,
I will live to bring You praise.

I believe in You,
Your grace has overwhelmed me.
I believe in You,
The lover of my soul.

1869

David Gate

I CAN SING WITH TONGUES OF ANGELS,
But if my life shows no love,
What have I?
I can understand Your greatness,
But if my life shows no love,
What have I?

Teach me to love,
Teach me to love like Jesus loved.

I can prophesy to nations,
But if my life shows no love,
What have I?
I can heal the sick and wounded,
But if my life shows no love,
What have I?

Open my eyes to see what You see.
Open my mind to be all that I can be.
Take my life and do what You will.
Teach me to love like Jesus loved.

1870

Tim & Rachel Hughes

I COULD LIVE A THOUSAND YEARS,
Never earn a moment of Your grace.
Even in my darkest day,
You shine on me, You shine on me.

And out of the darkness
You brought me into Your glorious light,
Saved from the death I was facing,
Rejoicing in the future hope that is mine.

The greatest of all gifts
From the greatest of all givers:
Jesus, there upon the cross,
True love displayed for all to see.

And Your grace runs after me,
Runs after me
Every day of my life.
And Your mercies, they never fail,
They never fail
Every day of my life.

Out of the darkness, out of the darkness.

1871

Chris Bowater

I COULD LOOK AT IMPERFECTION,
Feast my eyes on disappointment,
Fix my mind on constant failure
And never see what You see.
Looking through the eyes of mercy,
Washed by grace that cleanses vision,
Being changed by the love of Jesus,
I choose to see what You see.

A crown of beauty
In the hand of the Lord.
A royal diadem
In the hand of my God.
No longer forsaken,
No longer called desolate.
Now called the Lord's delight,
He rejoices over me.

I choose to see what You see,
Completing what's begun in me;
Renewing me, transforming me.

1872

Martyn Layzell & busbee

IF EVER I SHOULD FALTER,
If ever I should fall,
Your love is an anchor
And a refuge for my soul.
I build my world around You,
I'm building on the rock,
For only You are faithful,
Only You are strong.

And with Your grace I can face another day,
Run this race, holding on to You.
But when the road seems too hard to climb
I recall these words to mind:

Each new day, come what may, I'm pressing on,
With my eyes firmly fixed on You.
But when the load seems too much to bear,
On Your truth I can depend:

When all around me is shaking in this world, oh yeah,
Upon Your solid foundation I stand firm.

1873

Nick Herbert, John Peters & Pete Hughes

IF OUR GOD IS FOR US, who can be against?
He did not spare His own Son,
Stands at our defence.
Graciously He shines His face on us,
Powerful to heal and to restore.

If our God is for us,
Who can stand against us?
If our God is for us,

Who can stand against us?
If our God is for us,
Who can stand against us,
If our God is for us?

What can separate us from the love of Christ?
When hardship falls upon us,
Your grace will suffice.
Stronger than the power of death You are,
Greater than the one who's in this world.

We are more than conquerors
By Your Spirit within us.
We are more than conquerors
By Your Spirit within us.

1874

Tré & Tori Sheppard

IF YOU ARE WEARY,
Well, there is a rest here by His side.
If you are broken,
Well, there is healing by His side.

He is good, He is faithful, He is kind.
He is patient, He is loving, He is wise.
And He was willing to make the sacrifice,
So we will come and worship with our lives.

If you are hungry,
Well, there is truth here in His life.
If you are thirsty,
Well, there is love here in His eyes.

Come, let us adore Him;
Come, let us bow down.
(Repeat)

(Final chorus)
He is good, He is faithful, He is kind.
He is patient, He is loving, He is wise.
Lord, You were willing to make the sacrifice,
So we will come and worship with our lives.

1875

Evan Rogers

IF YOU HAD NOT HUMBLED YOURSELF for me
And died on the cross at Calvary,
There'd be no way that I could be free,
But Your precious blood
Has washed away my sin.

So I sing, I sing Your praises.
So I sing, I sing Your praises.

If You had not done what You had said:
That You would die then rise up from the dead,
There'd be no way that I could be saved
From the fear of death
And the power of the grave.

This is why we celebrate.
We celebrate Your incredible grace.
This is why we celebrate.
We celebrate Your incredible grace.

1876

Geraldine Latty

I GIVE MY LIFE TO YOU,
Knowing I can't do even one thing for You.
I give my life to You,
Knowing You have done
All that lets me come to You.

I bow my life down low,
Knowing I can't go through all You've been through.
I bow my life down low,
Knowing that is why
You have sacrificed Your life.

I look at You and see that I will never measure up.
You look at me and now I see I never have to.

I lift my praises high,
Knowing that the sky cannot hold Your glory.
I lift my praises high,
Knowing that one day
Every heart will say You are Lord.

1877

Andy Bromley, John Hartley & Susan Ashton

I GIVE UP, LAY IT DOWN,
Leave it all in the palm of Your hand.
Here I am, asking You:
Open my eyes to Your truth.
'Cause all that I need is in You,
All I desire is You.

You are everything:
My strength, my peace,
My joy, my hope.
In You I see everything.

Here I am on my knees,
Surrender to You all my fears.
Lift my eyes day to day,
Trusting in Your higher way.
'Cause all that I need is in You,
All I desire is You.

1878

Gareth Robinson

I HAVE NO ONE IN HEAVEN BUT YOU,
I want nothing on earth beside You,
For You alone are holy.
Lord, You alone are holy.

I have no one in heaven but You,
I want nothing on earth beside You,
For You alone are holy.
Lord, You alone are trustworthy.

So I will sing my praise to You,
For You are good, You are true.
No earthly thing compares to You.
Always faithful, ever-loving, mighty God.

And no one gives me life like You do.
No one gives me peace like You do.
No one gives me grace like You do.
No one gives me hope like You.

1879

Lex Loizides

I HAVE SEEN A MYSTERY,
The hopes of prayer and prophecy,
And rising from all peoples, see she comes.
Rescued, ransomed, lifted up,
Crowned with mercy, clothed in hope,
The object of all heaven's love, she comes.

It is the church,
The hope of all the world,
And here I fix my heart and hand,
I cannot turn away.
It is the church,

The passion of God's Son,
The goal of history,
Come, you'll see we've nearly reached the day.
And she will be all glorious;
Fitting for Him whose bride she is.

In that day, in that day.
In that day, in that day.

1880

Joel Houston & Jonathon Douglass

I LAY MY LIFE DOWN AT YOUR FEET,
You're the only One I need.
I turn to You and You are always there.
In troubled times it's You I seek,
I put You first, that's all I need.
I humble all I am, all to You.

One way, Jesus;
You're the only One that I could live for.
One way, Jesus;
You're the only One that I could live for.

You are always, always there,
Every how and everywhere;
Your grace abounds so deeply within me.
You will never, ever change;
Yesterday, today the same,
Forever, till forever meets no end.

You are the way, the truth and the life:
We live by faith and not by sight for You,
We're living all for You.

1881

Tim Hughes, Peter Furler & Steve Taylor

I LIFT UP MY VOICE to the King, the King of glory.
I hold out my hands to the One who is worthy.
I long for Your presence,
I long, Lord, I need Your touch.

Come, O Lord, and fill up my life
With the light of Your presence –
This is my heart's desire.
O Father, come and let Your Spirit abide,
I long for Your presence –
This is my heart's desire.

I long to be washed in the well of Your mercy.
I long to be warmed by the fire of Your glory.
I long for Your presence,
I long for Your healing touch.

It's my desire.
Lord, it's my desire.
Lord, You're my desire.
I want to feel Your presence,
I want to feel Your presence,
I want to feel Your presence, Jesus.

1882

Noel Robinson

I LOVE TO PRAISE YOUR NAME,
For You're ever the same,
The great I Am.
Our great deliverer reigns.
El Shaddai is Your name,
Strong and mighty to save.
The great deliverer is Your name.

Though I walk in the midst of trouble,
You will surround me.
Though my enemies encamp against me,
I shall not fear.
(Repeat)

1883

Noel Robinson & Donna Akodu

I LOVE YOU, LORD, with all my heart –
I felt this way right from the start.
I'm longing just to be with You.
Your love, it gives me a new song,
It lets me know that I belong.
It's Your love that keeps me day by day.

(Jesus, it is) Your love, eternal love,
Filling my heart with a new song.
(Jesus, it is) Your love, from above,
Let it reign.

Through darkest times, Lord, in my life,
You held my hands and gave me sight
To know within when I've done wrong.
And in the midst of all my pain,
You gave me strength to rise again;
Without Your love I can't go on.

Stronger, higher in You.
Your love gives me power,
I'm an overcomer in You.
Your love, overwhelming,
Overflowing, outpouring.
To the wounded, broken-hearted,
Pour out Your love today.
My Redeemer, love unending,
Saturating, never failing.
When I'm lonely and I'm hurting,
Pour out Your love today.

1884

Gareth Robinson

I LOVE YOU, LORD, WITH ALL OF MY HEART,
With all my emotions and feelings and dreams.
I love you, Lord, with all of my soul,
With all of my will and my conscious intent.

With everything within me, Lord,
Be glorified.
I love You, for You first loved me.

I love You, Lord, with all of my mind,
With every thought now made captive to You.
I love You, Lord, with all of my strength,
By putting to action the faith I profess.

And even when I fail, O Lord,
Your promise is secure.
Forgiving me as I forgive,
In Jesus I am Yours.

1885

Martyn Layzell

I'M AMAZED every day
At the newness of Your grace,
Like the dawn that awakes
To the song of morning sun.
Mercies new every morning.
Jesus, I give You glory:

I'll never stop loving You,
I'll never stop loving You.
All my days I'll sing Your praise,
I'll never stop loving You.

Swept away by the force
Of Your Spirit's burning flame,
Like a wave bound for shore
That will never cease to break.
Mercies new every morning.
Jesus, I give You glory:

You are love, You are grace,
Your compassions never fade.
You are joy in my pain,
You're the King of endless days.
Mercies new every morning.
Jesus, I give You glory:

1886

Stuart Townend

I'M COMING TO THE CROSS AGAIN,
The place where all the sin and shame
Of what I do
Was squarely placed on You.
The pressure's more than I can take;
I've tried to walk in my own strength,
I lay it down
Before Your thorny crown.

I've tried so hard to be someone
That You'd be proud to call Your son,
To earn the love
I know I don't deserve.
Yet when I think I'm standing tall,
The greater height, the bigger fall.
Now all I see
Is my futility.

But when You touch me,
I feel the burden slipping down again.
And when You touch me,
Can't stop the tears from falling down like rain.

I feel the shame of shallowness,
The kind of measured holiness
That seems to fit
The life I want to live.
How much of this is wood and straw?
I want to work for something more
Than piety,
Respectability.

And when the words cut like a knife
And harsh rejection haunts my life,
I tell myself
This was the pain You felt.
You walked this road a thousand times,
The victim of the cruellest crimes,
And left for dead
By every friend You had.

And when the accusations came
And You refused to play their game –
No words of hate
To set the record straight.
And when they taunted at the cross –
'If You are God, then save Yourself!'
You set Your face
To free this fallen race.

1887

Doug Horley

I'M GONNA JUMP UP AND DOWN,
Gonna spin right around,
Gonna praise Your name forever.

I'm gonna shout out loud,
Gonna deafen the crowd,
Gonna send my praise to heaven.
(Repeat)

I will run this race
And I will never stop.
I'll follow Jesus
Till the day I drop.
I can do all things
Through Christ who strengthens me.
When you've got such a lot,
When you've got not a lot,
What? Be happy!

1888

Martyn Layzell
Inspired by the William C. Smith (1824–1908) hymn

IMMORTAL, INVISIBLE, God only wise.
Love so accessible
Through the blood of Christ.
Most holy, most glorious, ancient of days,
Almighty, victorious,
Your great name we praise.
So we sing today:

Hallelujah, King forever,
You're the Name above all names.
Hallelujah, my Redeemer,
You are worthy of all praise.

We worship and honour You, Father of light,
While angels encircle You,
All veiling their sight.
Our praises we now declare, Father, to You,
And sing of the splendour
And glory that You're due.
So we sing today:

Most holy, most glorious,
Almighty, victorious.
(Repeat)

1889

Ian Hannah

I'M SO AMAZED by Your grace,
Pouring out from Your heart of love.
Precious Jesus, precious Saviour,
I'm so amazed by Your grace.
Can I find words to describe
What it meant when You gave Your life?
Precious Jesus, precious Saviour,
I'm so amazed by Your grace.

If You take away the power of the cross,
Where would I ever be?
If You take away the cleansing of Your blood,
I'd be lost for all eternity,
But You made the way for me.

1890

Darrell Evans

I'M TRADING MY SORROWS,
I'm trading my shame.
I'm laying them down
For the joy of the Lord.
I'm trading my sickness,
I'm trading my pain.
I'm laying them down
For the joy of the Lord.

I say, 'Yes, Lord, yes, Lord, yes, yes, Lord.
Yes, Lord, yes, Lord, yes, yes, Lord.
Yes, Lord, yes, Lord, yes, yes, Lord, amen.'

I am pressed but not crushed,
Persecuted not abandoned,
Struck down but not destroyed.
I am blessed beyond the curse,
For His promise will endure:
That His joy's gonna be my strength.
Though the sorrow may last for the night,
His joy comes with the morning.

1891

Tim Hughes

I NEVER KNEW A SWEETER NAME before.
No, I never knew a sweeter name before.
I never knew a sweeter name before.
No, I never knew a sweeter name before:

Than Jesus, Jesus Christ the Lord,
Jesus, Jesus Christ the Lord.
Jesus, Jesus Christ the Lord,
Than Jesus, Jesus Christ the Lord.

I never knew a greater name before . . .

1892

Noel Richards

IN HEAVEN AND EARTH
There is none like Him;
The Lord of lords,
The King of kings.
He came to earth
To die for us;
God raised Him up
Victorious.

Praise the Lord in all the earth,
Praise the Lord.
Praise the Lord in all the earth,
Praise the Lord.

We will worship with one voice,
In our King we will rejoice.
We will make His glory known.
Every nation, tribe and tongue,
They will know what He has done
When we make His glory known.

1893

Kate Simmonds

IN HIM I HAVE BELIEVED, on this my hope now rests,
That Jesus Christ is risen from the dead!
The all-surpassing joy
Of knowing Christ my Lord,
The former things, I count them all as loss.
Called out of darkness into Your goodness,
We are Your children, chosen in Christ.
Now in Your family, heirs of the promise,
To Your purpose on the earth I give my life.

A people born of God, united by Your call,
One faith, one Lord, one Father of us all.
Joined with bonds of love
And planted in Your house,
We worship You with hearts and lives poured out.
Let us go on in the power of Your Spirit,
Taking Your gospel to all the world,
Declaring Your wisdom, our great commission,
That Jesus Christ has come to save the lost.

Whatever trials may come, in faith, Lord, help us stand
For righteousness and justice in our land.
What fear can hold us now?
We run toward the prize,

Our lives already crucified with Christ.
Through every nation Your kingdom advances;
Who can extinguish this spreading flame?
Through tribulations we'll stand on Your promise:
'I will build My church and hell will not prevail!'

And on that final day, the citizens of heaven,
Called out to be the new Jerusalem,
In multitudes will bow
Before the throne of God:
One nation called from every tribe and tongue.
Great celebration! The glorious union:
The Lion of Judah and the pure, spotless bride.
All of creation waits for this moment,
All Your promises fulfilled in Jesus Christ.

1894

Mark Tedder

IN OUR DESPERATION
Heal our broken nations, God.
We are so determined
'Cause our hearts are burdened, God.

Bring Your fire to this land,
Heal our hearts with Your hand, O God.
Pray for peace in our nations,
This is our supplication, O God.

In this final hour
Show to us Your power, God.
May this generation
Go and shake the nations, God.

1895

Tim Hughes

IN THE BEGINNING,
Before You set the world in motion,
Uncreated, God eternal.
Radiant beauty, infinite,
The Godhead, three in one,
Perfect Father, Spirit, Saviour.

And it all begins and ends with You.
It all begins and ends with You,
The first and last,
The centre of it all.
And in You all things are held together –
Sun, the moon, the stars, the heavens –
Creator God,
The centre of it all.

All of the universe
Explodes in song before designer King,
Valley shaper, mountain maker.
The stars sing out;
They can't contain their praises of their God,
Earth creator, heaven shaker.

Beginning of it all,
The reason for it all,
The centre of it all.
(Repeat)

1896

David Gate

IN THE STILLNESS,
In the silence,
In the quiet of my heart,
I will listen for my Father
And the whispers of His heart.

Lord, I wait for You.
Lord, I wait for You.
I won't run, hide or move
Till I have met with You.

You're renewing, You're restoring,
My heart transforming day by day.
To pursue You, to adore You,
To be more like You in every way.

1897

Reuben Morgan

INTO YOUR HANDS I commit again
All that I am for You, Lord.
You hold my world in the palm of Your hand,
And I am Yours forever.

Jesus, I believe in You.
Jesus, I belong to You.
You're the reason that I live,
The reason that I sing
With all I am.

I'll walk with You wherever You go;
Through tears and joy I'll trust in You.
And I will live in all of Your ways
And Your promises forever.

I will worship, I will worship You.
I will worship, I will worship You.
(Repeat)

1898

Mark Beswick, Howard Francis & Clive McKinley

I OFFER UP TO YOU
Praises from my heart,
That they may be in truth
The perfect sacrifice.
To show my gratitude
For all the things You do,
I just want to give true praises from my heart.
Lord, I give to You true praises from my heart.

1899

Charlie Hall

I ONCE WAS FATHERLESS,
A stranger with no hope;
Your kindness wakened me,
Wakened me from my sleep.
Your love, it beckons deeply,
A call to come and die;
By grace now I will come and take this life,
Take Your life.

Sin has lost its power, death has lost its sting.
From the grave You've risen victoriously.

Into marvellous light I'm running –
Out of darkness, out of shame.
By the cross You are the truth,
You are the life, You are the way.

My dead heart now is beating,
My deepest stains now clean;
Your breath fills up my lungs,
Now I'm free, now I'm free.

Lift my hands and spin around,
See the light that I have found.
Oh, the marvellous light, marvellous light.

1900

Brooke Fraser

I SEE THE KING OF GLORY
Coming on the clouds with fire;
The whole earth shakes,
The whole earth shakes.
I see His love and mercy
Washing over all our sin;
The people sing,
The people sing:

Hosanna,
Hosanna,
Hosanna in the highest.
(Repeat)

I see a generation
Rising up to take their place,
With selfless faith,
With selfless faith.
I see a near revival
Stirring as we pray and seek;
We're on our knees,
We're on our knees.

Heal my heart and make it clean;
Open up my eyes to the things unseen.
Show me how to love
Like You have loved me,
Break my heart for what breaks Yours;
Everything I am for Your kingdom's cause,
As I walk from earth into eternity.

1901

Geraldine Latty

IT IS BY YOUR MIGHTY POWER
That we live and that we move.
It is by Your mighty power
That we breathe.
And in the name of Jesus risen,
By the Holy Spirit given,
It is by Your mighty power we believe.

And You're God above all rule and reign
And all authority.
Yet You have come to live in us,
And it is by Your mighty power we believe.

You enable us to walk,
Even in the darkest night,
And You equip us to be bearers of Your life.
We are salt and we are light,
We're already in the fight,
But it is by Your mighty power that we stand.

When the clouds are pushed aside,
And we move into that place
Where all the nations of the world will throw their crowns.
And as we gaze upon Your face
We will sing for endless days
That it's by Your mighty power that we've come.

1902

Geraldine Latty

IT'S AMAZING, *astounding, extravagant grace.* (x3)
Lord, to You I lift my praise.

In all my grieving and in all my weeping
Your grace still flows, Your grace still flows.
In all my seeking and on my returning
Your grace still flows to me.

In all my pain and through all my darkness
Your grace still flows, Your grace still flows.
In my indifference and through all my hardness
Your grace still flows to me.

Thank You for Your kindness,
That leads me to repentance.
Thank You for Your power,
That saves me, Jesus.
Thank You for Your name,
That lifts me to the Father.
What an amazing, extravagant grace!

In all my days of quiet restoring
Your grace still flows, Your grace still flows.
And when I walk with joy overflowing
Your grace still flows to me.

1903

Andy Bromley & Chris Donohue

IT'S FUNNY HOW Your words of life
Have turned me upside down,
And now I'm walking on this narrow road,
The road that leads me home.
It's funny how Your love came down
And changed me inside out,
And now I'm living my life differently:
I'm living for eternity.

And this kingdom's love beyond all loves,
This kingdom's joy in sorrow comes,
This kingdom's peace is given to me
Now freely to give.
This kingdom's hope, eternal life,
This kingdom's Son, the sacrifice.

This kingdom's cross,
This kingdom's blood,
Has paid the price for all to come.
And this kingdom,
And this kingdom.

1904

Graham Kendrick

I'VE COME TO WASH MY SOUL in the living water,
Wash my heart in Your cleansing stream.
Here is mercy and forgiveness;
I shall be clean again,
I shall be clean again.

I've come to bathe my eyes in Your word, Lord Jesus,
Cleanse my thoughts, my imaginings.
May these eyes see as Your love sees,
Light flood my being,
Light flood my being.

Oh, wash me whole in Your rushing river,
My Saviour.
Take me down to die and rise again.
(Repeat)

For I've been bought with the blood of Jesus,
Now my life is not my own.
A temple holy, for You only,
Where You are loved and known,
Where You are loved and known.

1905

Rex Allchurch

I'VE COME TO YOU so many times
With songs that are just words.
I sing them through
Without the heart,
But tell You they are true.

So help me, God, to live the life
That speaks through what I do,
That these are not just songs for church
But how I live for You.

I'll come back to the heart of why
These words are sung to You.
I'll sing them through
With all my heart
And live these words as truth.

So wash me now
And make me more like You.
Cleanse my heart so I can worship You.

1906

Tim Hughes

I'VE HAD QUESTIONS without answers,
I've known sorrow, I have known pain.
But there's one thing that I'll cling to:
You are faithful, Jesus, You're true.

When hope is lost, I'll call You Saviour.
When pain surrounds, I'll call You healer.
When silence falls,
You'll be the song within my heart.

In the lone hour of my sorrow,
Through the darkest night of my soul,
You surround me and sustain me;
My defender forever more.

I will praise You, I will praise You;
When the tears fall, still I will sing to You.
I will praise You, Jesus, praise You,
Through the suffering still I will sing.

1907

David Gate

I'VE PRAYED FOR THE FIRE,
I've prayed for the rain,
The power of God
In our land once again.

I look to the skies,
I fall on my knees,
Crying for more
Of Your mercies.

Let Your kingdom come,
Let Your will be done,
Let Your glory shine on the earth.

With courage and hope,
With faith and desire,
We'll cling to Your word
And pray for the fire.

To the ends of the earth,
To the ends of the earth,
To every corner of the world.
To the ends of the earth,
To the ends of the earth,
Let the name of Jesus be heard.

1908

Gareth Robinson

I WANT TO KNOW
Your pleasing and perfect will for me,
So renew my mind.
Open my eyes
So I can see the wonderful things
You have for me,
Amazing love.

Draw me nearer to You, Lord,
That I might know You more,
Faithful God.
Only You can satisfy:
Breathe on me Your breath of life,
'Cause all I want to do
Is be a living sacrifice for You.

And if I see You, I will know You.
And if I know You, then I will love like You.

1909

Andrew Mitchell

I WANT TO SING A SONG
Between just You and me.
Let all things fade away
As I draw near.
So fragile are my words,
But simply, Lord, I come,
For something deep inside
Needs Your love.

You are worthy of honour, glory and praise.
O High King of heaven, Jesus I pray:

Take my life away;
Pour in all of You.
Every part of me longs for more of You,
And my whole heart cries out, 'Worthy is my King.'

(First time)
Take my life away, take my life away.

(Second time)
You are holy.
Hallelujah, my God reigns.
Take my life away, take my life away,
Take my life away.

And now I take my cross
To carry in Your name,
And gladly I lay down
All earthly gains.
And bound in love with You,
My heart is truly free,
For I am one with Christ
And He is one with me.

1910

Gareth Paul Taylor

I WANT TO TELL YOU OF MY WONDER;
I stand in awe of You.
I want to tell You of Your beauty;
Your purity shines through.

Lord, I lose myself in Your presence,
And I lose myself in Your praise;
When I lose myself in You I'm found again.
Lord, I lose myself in Your presence,
And I lose myself in Your praise;
When I lose myself in You I find my way.

So many pressures are upon me
To take my eyes off You,
But You're my author and perfecter:
Come, write this day in You.

I want to tell You You are worthy
Of all that I can give.
I want to tell You You are lovely;
You made my Spirit live.

1911

Graham Kendrick & Tré Sheppard

I WILL ALWAYS LOVE THE LORD
With all of my heart.
I will always sing His praise
With all of my strength.
Through the bad times and the good
I've proved His love is true.

So honour the Lord with me,
(We honour You, Lord)
Honour the Lord with me.
(We honour You, Lord)
Let's celebrate a God so good, a God so great.
Honour the Lord with me,
(We honour You, Lord)
Honour the Lord with me.

I will always trust the Lord
With all of my heart.
I will place my hope in Him
With all of my strength.
He has been my hiding place
Whenever I feel afraid.

Come and taste, come and see,
Come broken in need
To this God of the poor,
The lost and the weak.
And our shame falls away
As our faces shine with His love.

1912

Miriam Webster

I WILL BLESS THE LORD FOREVER,
I will trust Him at all times.

He has delivered me from all fear,
He has set my feet upon a rock.
And I will not be moved,
And I'll say of the Lord:

You are my shield,
My strength, my portion, deliverer.
My shelter, strong tower,
My very present help in time of need.

Whom have I in heaven but You?
There's none I desire besides You.
And You have made me glad,
And I'll say of the Lord:

1913

Noel Robinson

I WILL GLORIFY YOUR NAME,
Glorify Your name.
I will glorify Your name in all the earth.

I will magnify Your name,
Magnify Your name.
I will magnify Your name in all the earth.

1914

Miriam Webster

I WILL LOVE YOU, LORD, my strength,
I belong to You;
And I will bless You while I live,
And I will lift my hands up in Your name.

Jesus, You alone are holy,
You alone are holy,
Name above every name.
Lord Jesus,
You alone are worthy,
You alone are worthy,
Jesus the Lamb that was slain.

Nailed to the cross for me,
Died and rose again,
You redeemed me to the Father:
By Your blood You cleansed me from all sin.

1915

Brenton Brown

I WILL NOT FORGET all Your benefits,
Even when the storm surrounds my soul;
How You comfort me, heal all my diseases;
How You lift me up on eagles' wings.

I will remember You,
Always remember You.
I will remember You
And all You've done for me.
(Repeat)

I will not forget all Your benefits;
How You've chosen and adopted me.
Orphaned by my sin, grace has let me in,
And never once have You abandoned me.

I have tasted and I've seen
How You father faithfully,
How You shepherd those who fear Your name.
When the shadows start to fall
And my heart begins to fail,
I will lift my eyes to You again.

1916

Godfrey Birtill

I WILL SET MY FACE *to seek the Lord.*
I will set my face to seek the Lord,
Give my full attention to my God;
I will listen for His voice,
I will listen for His voice.

My wonderful counsellor,
My teacher, reminder,
Revealer, my healer,
My strengthener, repairer,
Refiner, my Jesus, my Saviour,
My wonderful God.
Forerunner and finisher,
My conqueror, deliverer,
Restorer, my hammer,
My fire, uniter,
Redeemer, my Jesus,
My wonderful God.

Creator, defender,
My maker, instructor,
Commander, my warrior,
My shelter, my helper,

My leader, my Jesus, my Saviour,
My wonderful God.
My shepherd, my gatherer,
Refresher, rewarder,
Protector, inspirer,
Provider, my portion,
Forever, my Jesus, my Saviour,
My wonderful God.

1917

John Hartley & Chris Eaton

I WILL TRUST IN YOU, Lord, with all of my heart,
With all of my mind and soul.
And in all of my ways acknowledge You
As Saviour and Lord of all.

*May the words of my mouth
And my every thought
Be pleasing to You, O God.
And may I always bring
A worshipful heart,
Surrendered forever to You.*

I will trust in You, Lord, and I shall not want –
You're all I could ever need.
So come lay me down in pastures green
And into my life bring Your peace.

1918

Geraldine Latty & busbee

JESUS CHRIST – PERFECT LOVE,
Holy One that knows no fault,
Screen my thoughts, make me clean,
Know the motives of my heart.

When I see my selfish choice,
When I glimpse Your holiness,
Then I realise again
Perfect love has come to cleanse.

Jesus Christ – Lord for all,
Plant in me the kingdom seed.
Search me, Lord, when I'm found
Looking only to my needs.
When I see the way You lived,
How You dignified the poor,
Then I realise again
How I need to know You more.

Jesus Christ – Lamb of God,
Love resolved to take our place:
Who can write or describe
All of Your self-giving grace?
When I look at the brutal cross,
Innocence and beauty slain,
That's when I realise once more
You fully understand our pain.

Jesus Christ – King of heaven,
Qualified to wear the crown.
In Your face, radiant grace
Draws us closer to Your throne.
When we see Your generous heart,
When we touch the world You love,
That's when we realise again:
Perfect love is perfect hope.

1919

Charlie Hall

JESUS, COME TAKE ME AWAY;
I long to see Your face.
And this world is broken, yet beautifully made;
Jesus, come take me away.

Jesus, I'll patiently wait,
Till like a vapour I'll fade.
Help me fulfil all Your dreams for these days;
Jesus, I'll patiently wait.

You'll come again with a shout,
Like a thief in the night
You'll come riding on clouds.
Finally the voice I had followed for life
Has a glorious face that is lit up with light.

And You'll come to me.
No more pain, peace.
No more fear, release.
Just lost and consumed with my glorious King.

Jesus, today I am tired.
I need Your music to come and inspire me.
I give myself to be refined in this fire;
But Jesus, today I'm so tired.

Come to me, come to me.

1920

Keith Getty & Steve Siler

JESUS, EVER ABIDING FRIEND,
My soul's rest and journey's end;
Blameless One, who erased my sin
For eternity.

Comfort through my deepest pain,
Love that sees beyond my shame;
Christ, the sweetest, dearest name
That my heart has ever known.

Jesus, Saviour, with crown of thorns,
My soul's peace forever more;
Constant, caring, redeeming Lord,
Life abundantly.
Rock of heaven, strength and shield,
Perfect holiness revealed:
Christ by whom my wounds were healed,
Name above all other names.

1921

Matt Redman

JESUS, I COULD SING
In the tongues of men and angels,
But if I have not love
I am just a clanging cymbal, an empty sound.
(Repeat)

> *This is a love song,*
> *This is a love song,*
> *Jesus, a love song to You.*
> *A song of devotion, a reverent passion,*
> *Saviour, a love song to You.*

And Jesus, I could pray
With a faith that moves a mountain,
But if I have not love
It is just a noise resounding, an empty sound.
(Repeat)

It's the overflow of hearts
As we gaze upon Your beauty;
A reflection of Your worth,
For we've seen a glimpse of You in Your glory, Lord.
(Repeat)

1922

Steve Merkel

JESUS, I'VE FORGOTTEN
The words that You have spoken;
Promises that burned within my heart
Have now grown dim.
With a doubting heart I follow
The paths of earthly wisdom;
Forgive me for my unbelief,
Renew the fire again.

Lord, have mercy.
Christ, have mercy.
Lord, have mercy on me.
Lord, have mercy.
Christ, have mercy.
Lord, have mercy on me, on me.

I have built an altar
Where I worship things of man;
I have taken journeys
That have drawn me far from You.
So now I am returning
To Your mercies ever flowing;
Pardon my transgressions,
Help me love You again.

I have longed to know You
And all Your tender mercies,
Like a river of forgiveness
Ever flowing without end.
So I bow my heart before You
In the goodness of Your presence,
Your grace forever shining
Like a beacon in the night.

1923

David Holmes & Darlene Zschech

JESUS, JESUS, HOLY ONE,
God's precious Son, You gave.
Jesus, Jesus,
On the cross You took my shame;
Forever from my heart I'll say:

I live to worship You, Lord,
My King of glory.
Brought me to life,
Gave me wings to fly:
You are holy.
Heaven and earth
Declare Your praise.
Both now and evermore
I glorify Your name.

Jesus, Jesus,
On the cross You took my sin;
Forever from my heart I'll sing:

1924

J. M. Harris (1867–1934)
Adpt. words & new music by Andy Bromley

JESUS, MY KING, my wonderful Saviour,
All of my life is given to Thee.
Now I am living in Your great salvation,
Your precious blood is making me free.

Wonderful Saviour, wonderful Saviour,
You are so near, so precious to me.
Wonderful Saviour, wonderful Saviour,
My heart is filled with praises to Thee.

Freedom from sin, Oh wonderful story,
All of its stains washed whiter than snow.
Jesus has come to live in this temple;
All of my days His love I will show.

Jesus my Lord, I'll ever adore Thee,
Lay at Your feet my treasures of love.
Lead me in ways to show forth Your glory,
Ways that will end in heaven above.

When in that bright and beautiful city,
There I will see Your glories untold.
I will be like You, my wonderful Saviour;
I will sing praise while ages unfold.

1925

Doug Williams & Andrew Small

JESUS, NAME ABOVE ALL NAMES,
Let all creation sing out Your praise.
You're my only desire,
Loving You deeper each passing day.

In times of trouble, Lord, You rescue me,
My shelter from the storm.
It's in Your name that I will put my trust;
You're with me through it all.

In Your name I will stand,
From the curse of sin set free.
In Your name I will fight;
Darkness has no hold on me
In Your name, in Your name.

Jesus, beautiful Saviour,
Tower of refuge, my hiding place.
I'd be so lost without You,
Your tender mercy, amazing grace.

In Your name we put our trust.
All we need to do is ask, Lord,
In Your name.

1926

Gareth Robinson

JESUS, SAVIOUR,
I bring my pain, You bring Your healing.
Trading, sharing,
For by Your wounds and in Your love I'm healed.

Jesus, Saviour,
I bring my sin, You bring forgiveness.
Trading, sharing,
Your death has brought fullness of life to me.

So here I stand,
Saved by Your blood,
Bought with a price
And learning to live in the victory.
And this I will say for all of my days:
'Jesus saved and is still saving me.'

Jesus, Saviour,
I bring my fears, You bring Your peace.
Trading, sharing,
Your perfect love fulfils my deepest need.

(For) one day I'll be whole,
And one day I'll be pure,
On that day when You're revealed
As King of kings and Lord of lords.

1927

Graham Kendrick

JESUS, THE SOURCE OF ALL OUR JOY,
Full of truth and grace;
The Father's living, breathing Word –
What more could He say?
Pour out the passion of Your heart
That sent You from above,
To know the Father and make known
His amazing love.

Our God, whom none has ever seen,
You have brought so near;
The beating heart of love divine,
Close enough to hear.
And in Your words we hear a voice
That puts our fear to flight;
The Father singing over us
Songs of pure delight.

And my heart yearns for You.
And my heart yearns for You.

How can we ever comprehend
All Your blood has bought?
You made a way for us to share
The very life of God.
To know the love that burned for You
Before the world began,
And by Your power to become
God's own children.

We hear the passion of Your prayer
That we may be one,
So all the world may believe
You have truly come.

Teach us to love with that same love
That sent You from above;
To know the Father and make known
His amazing love.

1928

Brenton Brown & Don Williams

JESUS, YOU ARE MERCY,
Jesus, You are justice,
Jesus, You are worthy,
That is what You are.
You died alone to save me,
You rose so You could raise me;
You did all this to make me
A chosen child of God.

Worthy is the Lamb that once was slain
To receive all glory, power and praise,
For with Your blood You purchased us for God:
Jesus, You are worthy,
That is what You are.

Perfect sacrifice,
Crushed by God for us,
Bearing in Your hurt all that I deserve.
Misjudged for my misdeeds,
You suffered silently,
The only guiltless man in all of history.

1929

Gareth Robinson

JESUS, YOU HUMBLED YOURSELF
To death on a cross.
You rose from the grave
And now, Jesus,

You're King of all kings
And Lord of all lords,
And only in You are we saved.

In Your name there is healing.
In Your name there is peace.
In Your name there is salvation,
For Your name is love.

1930

Keith & Kristyn Getty & Ian Hannah

JESUS, YOUR NAME, Prince of Peace,
Quiets my soul, treasures the least.
In perfect rest You will keep
All whose hope is in You.
Jesus, Your name can silence the storms,
The strivings that trouble our world.
Jesus, Your name reveals You as Lord:
O, powerful name!

Jesus, Your name, counsellor,
Wonderful way, life's comforter.
Spirit of truth defending me,
Though in me was the blame.
Jesus, Your name has stood in my place
And freed me from hopeless shame.
Jesus, Your name now fathers me:
With joy I bear His name.

Jesus, Your name, mighty God,
All-powerful One ruling in love.
There is a King upon the throne
Earth cannot overthrow.
Jesus, Your name, great banner of hope,
Steadies the knees of the weak.
Jesus, the name all nations will praise:
O, glorious name!

1931 Stuart Townend & Keith Getty

JOY HAS DAWNED UPON THE WORLD,
Promised from creation:
God's salvation now unfurled,
Hope for every nation.
Not with fanfares from above,
Not with scenes of glory,
But a humble gift of love:
Jesus born of Mary.

Sounds of wonder fill the sky
With the songs of angels,
As the mighty Prince of life
Shelters in a stable.
Hands that set each star in place,
Shaped the earth in darkness,
Cling now to a mother's breast,
Vulnerable and helpless.

Shepherds bow before the Lamb,
Gazing at the glory;
Gifts of men from distant lands
Prophesy the story:
Gold, a King is born today;
Incense, God is with us;
Myrrh, His death will make a way,
And by His blood He'll win us.

Son of Adam, Son of heaven,
Given as a ransom
Reconciling God and man,
Christ our mighty champion!
What a Saviour, what a friend,
What a glorious mystery:
Once a babe in Bethlehem,
Now the Lord of history.

1932

Matt Redman

JOY IS THE THEME of my song
And the beat of my heart,
And that joy is found in You.
For You showed the power of Your cross
And Your great saving love,
And my soul woke up to You.
I heard Your beautiful news,
Grace so amazing, so true.

Shout it out, let the people sing;
Something so powerful
Should shake the whole wide world.
Make it loud, make it louder still;
Saviour, we're singing now
To celebrate Your beautiful news.

There's a God who came down to save,
Showed the world His amazing grace.
There's a God who came down to save,
And He calls your name.

1933

Brenton Brown

JUST LIKE THE ONES who came before us,
Just like the ones who gave their lives,
Lord, we will leave this place with You
And we will go, we will go.
Just as You came to earth from heaven,
Humbled Yourself, gave Your life,
We want to follow and obey You,
So we will go, we will go.

Light of the world, You shone on us,
You filled our hearts
With hope that reaches out.

Friend of the world, Saviour to me,
Make me a flame, set me on fire,
To be a light in the world.

Just as they prayed to You for power,
That they'd be bold to speak Your word,
Father, we ask that You would fill us
As we go, as we go.
Just as they asked You for salvation,
Just as they prayed for kingdom signs,
Lord, would You send us with Your Spirit
As we go, as we go, we want to go?

Set me on fire, Lord, make me a flame.
Release revival – please do it again.
(Repeat)

1934

Andy Smith

KING OF ALL and yet You came,
You gave it all away, gave it all away.
Chose the cross, You took my blame,
And gave Yourself away, gave Yourself away.

So this is how I know it's true:
It's not about me, it's about You.
I'm faceless, hidden in Your love,
A nameless warrior I'll become.

Jesus, You are awesome.
You bridged the gap for me
And what You've done will last forever.
You took the hope of glory
And set it deep inside me;
You reign supreme over all the earth.

You made a call on me today
To give it all away, give it all away.
A promise I have made today,
Not just the words I say,
I'll give it all away.

1935

Paul Oakley

KING OF ANGELS, King of saints,
King of all creation praise.
King of lost and King of found,
King who wore my thorny crown.
Crucified to set me free,
King of glory, now my eyes can see
Your majesty.

And I praise You, I praise You,
I praise You, I praise You for all eternity.
I will sing, I will sing, I will sing,
I will sing to You, Jesus, my King.

King of sunshine, King of rain,
King of all my waking days.
King in joy and King through pain,
You will always be the same.
Sing aloud, my soul awake,
Sing of His unfailing love and grace
All my days.

All heaven shines with You
As angel eyes behold Your face.
No one else compares with You,
So I bow in awe of You.

1936

Al Gordon

KING OF GLORY, King of light,
I see You, I see You.
Shining in the face of Christ,
Your beauty illuminates
With brilliance brighter than the sun.

You are the One I love,
You're glorious, glorious.
You have won my heart,
You're glorious, glorious.

Face to face, my life unveiled,
I worship, I worship You.
You're my everlasting light,
Your glory captivates
With brilliance brighter than the sun.

And I won't turn my eyes away.
No, I won't turn my eyes away.
(Repeat)

1937

Keith Getty & Stuart Townend

LET THE EARTH RESOUND with songs of praise
To the Father's power and love,
For the One who set each star in place
Chose to set His heart on us.
To the One whose might gives victory,
Yet whose mercies never cease,
As the tapestry of history
Tells the story of His grace.

King immortal, faithful God,
Crowned with splendour, rich in love,
Let the heavens and the earth resound
With songs of praise to You.

Let the earth be stilled before the sight
Of a Father's sacrifice,
That revealed the depths of love divine
In the face of Jesus Christ.
Through a life of full obedience
And a death in agony,
He removed the rebel's punishment
And He set the prisoner free.

Let the earth resound with songs of faith
At the wonder yet to come,
When all sin and pain are put to death
And the church and Christ are one.
When we stand as God's great family
And we meet the Father's gaze,
And we share in His eternal joy
As we join in ceaseless praise:

1938

Brenton Brown

LET US COME TOGETHER,
Let us join as one;
Let us turn our faces
To the rising sun.
Let us go up to Zion,
To God's holy hill:
A mighty army that will worship Him.

We will worship Him.
We will worship Him.
Jesus, He's our King,
We will worship Him.

Let the oceans roar,
Let the heavens ring
To the glory of our God
As we worship Him.

It is time for battle,
It is time for war,
As we sing hosanna,
As we praise the Lord.
He will still the accuser,
Crush the enemy,
As we celebrate God's victory.

1939

Matt Redman

LET WORSHIP BE THE FUEL for mission's flame,
We're going with a passion for Your name;
We're going, for we care about Your praise.
Send us out.

Let worship be the heart of mission's aim
To see the nations recognise Your fame.
Till every tribe and tongue voices Your praise,
Send us out.

You should be the praise of every tongue,
You should be the joy of every heart.
Until the fullness of Your kingdom comes,
And till that final revelation dawns,
Send us out.

Every tribe, every tongue,
Every creature in the heavens and the earth,
Every heart, every soul
Will sing Your praise, will sing Your praise.
Every note, every string,
Every melody will be for You alone,

Every harmony that flows from every tongue
Will sing Your praise, will sing Your praise,
Will sing Your praise, will sing Your praise.

1940

Chris Tomlin & Jesse Reeves

LIFT UP YOUR GAZE, be lifted up,
Tell everyone how great the love,
The love come down from heaven's gate
To kiss the earth with hope and grace.

Sing: Who is this King of glory?
The Lord, strong and mighty!
(Repeat)

Lift up your hands, be lifted up,
Let the redeemed declare the love.
And we bow down at heaven's gate
To kiss the feet of hope and grace.

There is one God; He is holy.
There is one Lord over everything.
There is one King; He is Jesus,
King of glory, strong and mighty!

(Last chorus)
You are the King of glory.
The Lord, strong and mighty!

1941

James Montgomery (1771–1854)
Adpt. Godfrey Birtill

LIFT UP YOUR HEADS, you gates of brass,
You bars of iron, yield,
And let the King of glory pass;
The cross is in the field.

Alleluia, alleluia, alleluia, alleluia,
Alleluia, alleluia, alleluia, alleluia.

You armies of the living God,
Stand in your Captain's might.
Go where no hallowed feet have trod;
Arise, My warrior bride.

O fear not, faint not, halt not now.
Don't quit: like men, be strong.
To Christ shall every nation bow
And sing with you this song.

Uplifted are the gates of brass,
The bars of iron yield.
Behold the King of glory pass;
The cross has won the field.

1942

Keith & Kristyn Getty

LIGHT OF GOD, come dwell within Your people,
As intended from the dawn of time.
Make Your goodness, echoed through creation,
Our desire, Joy of the Divine.

Holy Spirit, break through our darkness;
Holy Spirit, breathe through our lives.
Light of God, come, radiant and glorious;
Perfect wisdom in this world today.

Light of God, come to Your fallen people,
As we follow in the steps of Christ.
May Your fragrance beautify Your people,
As we mirror our Creator's light.

Light of God, come claim Christ's stolen glory,
Burn the shadows with the flame of truth.
May Your church rise, stars within the darkness,
Giving glory to the Lord of light.

Light divine, come, Father of all beauty;
Son of goodness, Spirit of all truth.
Move us, use us, people of Your vision,
As we wait for our returning King.

1943

Dave Bilbrough

LIKE A MIGHTY RIVER,
A pure and healing stream,
Grace flows from the Saviour
To wash the guilty clean.
There's nothing we can offer,
No deed will ever earn;
The gift of His forgiveness
Is free and undeserved.

1944

Brenton Brown

LIKE A WHISPER, like a love song,
I can hear Your voice, I can hear Your voice.
Like a father to his newborn,
I can hear Your voice calling me:

You are My child;
You are My child and I love you.
(Repeat)

Like a promise, like a thank you,
I will sing this song, I will sing this song.
For the way You make my heart new,
I will sing this song to You:

You are my God,
You are my God and I love You.
(Repeat)

There is no higher call,
There's no greater reward
Than to know You, God,
To be known as Yours.
There is no better goal;
Nothing I'm longing for
Can compare with the truth
That forever more:

1945

Geraldine Latty

LONG BEFORE WE WERE CREATED,
At the dawn of space and time,
God eternal, great and mighty
Had us on His mind.
He devised and set before us
An amazing, perfect plan
That would demonstrate to all
The giving of His hand.

Praise God, praise God,
Our God who saves.
Praise God, praise God,
Who calls us to magnify
The glory of His grace.

We're a part of His own family
Simply through the love of Christ.
What a perfect, all-embracing,
Selfless sacrifice.
God has thought of every option,
He's provided all we need;
That the weak, the strong, the rich,
The poor can know His peace.

This is our Father's story,
This is our maker's praise,
And by the Spirit
We're the story of His grace.
Using ordinary people,
Using broken jars of clay,
He'll display the grace
That even death can't take away.

1946

Godfrey Birtill & Martin Scott

LOOKING FOR YOUR PRESENCE,
It's time to seek Your face.
May the windows of heaven open up today.
Let us flow with Your rhythm,
The Spirit and the word,
Pick up Your burdens,
Walk the land and pray.

Carrying You, carrying You
Into the city streets and homes.
Carrying You, carrying You,
We hear the footsteps of the Lord.

Can Your heavy glory,
Can Your heavy glory,
Can Your heavy glory rest on me?
(Repeat)

1947

Nathan Fellingham & Paul Oakley

LOOKING IN THE SKY,
Whoever could deny Your glory?
Gazing into space,
How small the human race appears.

Seeing You in all Your majesty,
I wonder how it could be
That You delight in me.

Lord, You are an amazing God.
Lord, You are an amazing God.
Lord, You are an amazing God,
And I love You, I love You.

Lord of everything,
No other god or king is like You.
Powerful and strong,
Yet tender is Your song to me.
Knowing the extent of all my sin,
However could You be pleased
To pour Your love on me?

You light up the heavens with just one word,
You measure the mountains in Your hand;
Yet You treasure the broken and make them whole,
You crown us with Your love.

1948

Tré & Tori Sheppard

LORD, HERE WE ARE,
Sons and daughters of Your hand;
Here, waiting for You
With our hearts and with our plans.
So come, fill us with faith,
Fill us with peace once again.
Come, fill us with hope,
Fill us with wonder and with love.

You are the One,
You are the One,
You are the One,
Only One.

All of my heart, all of my soul,
All of my treasure is in You.
All that I search for, all that I found,
All that I wanted is in You,
It's in You.

1949

Andrew Mitchell

LORD, I BRING TO YOU ALL THAT I AM;
I can come to You no other way.
But I see in Your heart all the love that I need;
Let it come down upon me.

Lord, I give to You all of my heart,
And I know that I've said it before;
But this time that I give, I hold nothing back,
And give to You all that I am.

Father, hear my cry, come and fill my life
With all You have to give.
Take all that I am in Your Father's hands;
To be like Jesus is all that I ask.

Lord, I pray You'll be with me each day,
And I pray You'll be there when I fall;
Through my trials and my joys
Let Your love remain
Everlasting and always the same.

And let these words I sing be an offering,
Reaching the height of Your throne.
Lord, I'm Yours, You are mine;
O Lord, I'm Yours and You are mine.

1950

LORD, I STILL BELIEVE in all You promised,
Though I'm tired of hanging on.
Draw me to my knees so I'll be honest;
I'm still breaking to be whole.
So I come to You again,
Yes, I come to You again.

You give hope and life to everyone,
You give dreams and grace where there is none.
Jesus, I'm free.
You give songs to the broken-hearted,
You take guilt from the heavy-minded.
Jesus, I'm free.

Lord, do You still hear all that I promise,
Though I'm tired of holding on?
So I'm kneeling at Your rugged cross
And offering my rugged soul.

And it's You I sing for, You and You alone.
Yes, it's You I sing for, You and You alone.
(Repeat)

1951

LORD, THIS HEART MUST SING
Of all that You have done for me:
The beauty of the cross,
The greatness of Your loss.

So I'll thank You for the day
When You washed my sin away.

I will never lose the wonder
Of the blood You shed for me.
There could be no greater love than this
Through all eternity.
So I'll thank You for the day
When You washed my sin away.

Help me understand
Just what it meant for You, Jesus:
The holy King of all,
Upon a sinner's cross.

1952

Godfrey Birtill

LORD, TURN YOUR FOOTSTEPS
Towards these ruins.
We need You here,
We need You here.
Our homes are broken
And our children get stolen.
We need You here,
We need You here.

Our God and King,
Ancient of Days,
Alpha, Omega, Jesus, Saviour,
Work Your deliverance in this place.
Yours is the night,
Yours is the day.
No one is greater.
Come, Lord, save us,
Work Your deliverance in this place.

Lord, turn Your footsteps
Towards these ruins.
We need You here,
We need You here,

(In these) streets filled with darkness,
With our children fatherless.
We need You here,
We need You here.

1953

Matt Redman

LORD, WE HAVE SEEN the rising sun
Awakening the early dawn,
And we're rising up to give You praise.
Lord, we have seen the stars and moon,
See how they shine, they shine for You,
And You're calling us to do the same.
So we rise up with a song
And we rise up with a cry,
And we're giving You our lives.

We will shine like stars in the universe,
Holding out Your truth in the darkest place.
We'll be living for Your glory,
Jesus, we'll be living for Your glory.
We will burn so bright with Your praise,
O God,
And declare Your light to this broken world.
We'll be living for Your glory,
Jesus, we'll be living for Your glory.

Like the sun so radiantly
Sending light for all to see,
Let Your holy church arise.
Exploding into life
Like a supernova's light,
Set Your holy church on fire.

So we rise up with a song
And we rise up with a cry,
And we're giving You our lives:
Jesus, we will shine.

1954

Mark Beswick & Howard Francis

LORD, WE LOVE TO PRAISE YOU,
Lord, to magnify Your name.
What a privilege,
A privilege to praise.

O Lord, O Lord,
O Lord, O Lord, O Lord.
What a privilege,
A privilege to praise.

1955

Stuart Townend & Keith Getty

LORD, WE WAIT for the day of Your appearing;
Lord, we wait for Your coming in the clouds.

With a shout the trumpet will sound
And the dead will be raised to life,
And we shall meet Him in the air!

In that day death is swallowed up in victory;
In that day sin and death shall be no more.

1956

Joel Houston

(With all my heart I'll say,
I'm living for Your name,
With all to give You praise,
I'm living for Your glory, Lord.)

LOST FOR WORDS, with all to say:
Lord, You take my breath away.
Still my soul, my soul cries out,
For You are holy.

And as I look upon Your name
Circumstances fade away,
And now Your glory steals my heart,
For You are holy.
You are holy, You are holy, Lord.

Evermore my heart, my heart will say:
Above all I live for Your glory.
Even if my world falls I will say:
Above all I live for Your glory.
Above all I live for Your glory.

1957

Bryn Haworth

LOVE CAME DOWN at Christmas time,
Love all lovely, love divine.
Star and angels gave the sign:
Love came down for us.

Born into a time of war,
Choosing to be with the poor,
Our Saviour on a bed of straw,
Love came down for us.

'Glory in the highest,'
Hear the angels sing;
'Peace on earth to all mankind,
On whom His favour rests.'

Clothed in frail humanity,
To this world that we might see
The greatest gift in history:
Love came down for us.

In the darkness light still shines,
Bringing hope to all mankind.

Love be yours and love be mine;
Love came down for us.
Love came down for us.

Jesus, Saviour, Name above all names.
Wonderful Counsellor, Prince of Peace,
Mighty God.

1958

Keith Getty & Stuart Townend

LOVE OF GOD, revealed in wonder
By the works of a maker's hand;
Seas that roar with thunderous splendour,
Fields that whisper at His command.
All the joys of life we cherish
Are God's gracious sign
We are children of His promise,
Heirs of mercy and grace divine.

Unfailing love from heaven's throne,
That sought me out and brought me home.
My song of praise shall ever be:
The Father's love for me.

Love of God, revealed in frailty,
Through the gift of a servant King;
Joy of heaven robed in humility,
Prince of Peace crowned with suffering.
Oh, what love, that calls humanity
To kneel at the cross
And exchange our sin's futility
For the joy of a father's love.

Love of God, what priceless treasure
Over all this world affords:
To be His and His forever,
This my glory and my reward!

May this love beyond all knowing
So capture my soul
That I'm filled to overflowing
With a passion for Him alone!

1959

Robert Critchley

LOVE THAT CLEANSES all my stains,
Love that makes me whole again;
Love forgiving, setting free,
Love of God, wash over me.

Your healing love,
Your healing love
Flowing down like a river over me.

Love that showers mercy sweet,
Love that washes sinners' feet;
Love that makes my life complete,
Love of God, wash over me.

Pouring over me,
Pouring over me,
Pouring over me;
O Jesus, I receive.

1960

Joel Houston & Marty Sampson

LOVE UNFAILING,
Overtaking my heart.
You take me in,
Finding peace again;
Fear is lost in all You are.

And I would give the world to tell Your story,
'Cause I know that You've called me,
I know that You've called me.
I've lost myself for good within Your promise,
And I won't hide it,
I won't hide it.

'Cause Jesus, I believe in You,
And I would go to the ends of the earth,
To the ends of the earth.
For You alone are the Son of God,
And all the world will see that You are God,
That You are God.

1961

Chris Bowater

MAGNIFICENT, ALL GLORIOUS LORD.
Omnipotent, victorious,
Sovereign Master, King forever.
Most marvellous, all radiant God.
In excellence pre-eminent,
Sovereign Master, King forever.

Your thoughts to bless: unlimited.
Surpassing grace, transcending love,
You are in all Your ways most wonderful;
And all Your ways are ever sure and true
In all You do.

1962

Paul Oakley

MAJESTY AND PRAISE
Ever shall belong to You.
Every star in the sky
Ever lives to shine for You.

No other god shall share Your fame,
No other song outlive Your praise.

You reign forever,
Jesus, my Saviour, my God.
I'm living every day for Your name.
For all eternity
You'll be my hope and my song;
I lift my voice to crown You with praise.

Never-ending grace
Ever draws me to Your throne.
Every breath that I take
Shall be Yours and Yours alone.
No other god shall share Your fame,
No other song outlive Your praise.

1963

Reuben Morgan

MAY OUR HOMES BE FILLED WITH DANCING,
May our streets be filled with joy;
May injustice bow to Jesus
As the people turn and pray.

From the mountain to the valley,
Hear our praises rise to You.
From the heavens to the nations,
Hear the singing fill the air.

May a light shine in the darkness
As we walk before the cross;
May Your glory fill the whole earth,
As the water o'er the seas.

Hallelujah, hallelujah,
Hallelujah, hallelujah.
(Repeat)

1964

Stuart Townend & Keith Getty

MAY THE PEACE OF GOD our heavenly Father,
And the grace of Christ the risen Son,
And the fellowship of God the Spirit
Keep our hearts and minds within His love.

And to Him be praise for His glorious reign,
From the depths of earth to the heights of heaven.
We declare the name of the Lamb once slain:
Christ eternal, the King of kings!

May this peace which passes understanding,
And this grace which makes us what we are,
And this fellowship of His communion
Make us one in spirit and in heart.

1965

Andrew Mitchell

MEET WITH US, LORD, in Your tabernacle
And pour out Your Spirit, we pray.
Let this sanctuary be so holy and fragrant,
And filled with the sound of our praise.
We gather round Your throne room
And enter in as we cry:

Holy Lord, our King of kings,
Lord of power and of might.
Let all the earth rejoice
With the bride of Christ,
Singing majesty and hosanna
To our Lord on high.

Lord of all life, our wonderful Saviour,
We are Your garment of praise.
Let this anthem of love soar like a heart's cry

That welcomes You here in this place, Jesus.
We see You robed in splendour
Above all things, and we cry:

Exalting You, Lord Jesus,
We raise our hands.
Come riding on Your white horse:
Behold the Lamb!

1966

Keith & Kristyn Getty & Stuart Townend

MERCIFUL GOD, O abounding in love,
Faithful to all who draw near You;
Hearing the cries of the humble in heart,
Showing the cross they may cling to.
Helpless I come, broken in sin,
Found at the feet of Your mercy.
Father, forgive,
May my sin be remembered no more.

Merciful God, O abounding in love,
Faithful through times we have failed You –
Selfish in thought and uncaring in deed,
Foolish in word and ungrateful.
Spirit of God, conquer our hearts
With love that flows from forgiveness;
Cause us to yield
And return to the mercy of God.

Merciful God, O abounding in love,
Faithful to keep us from falling;
Guiding our ways with Your fatherly heart,
Growing our faith with each testing.
God speed the day struggles will end,
Faultless we'll gaze on Your glory;
Then we will stand
Overwhelmed by the mercy of God.

1967

Chris Eaton & John Hartley

MOST HOLY FATHER, I come to You,
Knowing that You alone,
You can make me whole.
My precious Jesus, I long for You
To make my heart a dwelling place
For Your love.

For You alone are holy, bountiful in mercy,
Forever You are worthy to receive the glory.

And I believe in You,
Ruler over everything.
The wonders of my God and King
Shine over all the earth.
And I believe in You,
My Saviour, You're amazing.
Your love is never ending,
And I believe in You.

Thankful, so thankful, I come to You,
Knowing that You alone have made a way for me.
Faithful, so faithful, You are to me,
Steadfast and certain is Your love.

1968

Chris Tomlin, Michael John Clement & Jesse Reeves

MOUNTAIN-MAKER, ocean-tamer,
Glimpses of You burn in my eyes.
The worship of heaven
Fills up the skies.

You made it all,
Said 'Let there be',
And there was all that we see.

The sound of Your voice,
The works of Your hands,
You do all things well,
You do all things well,
You do all things well.

Star-creator, wind-breather,
The strokes of Your beauty
Brushed through the clouds,
Light from the heavens
Touching the ground.

Imagination runs wild
And breathes the breath of life
Across the fields, across the miles.

1969

Stuart Townend

MY GOD, full of mercy,
Heard our weeping,
Came to bring us home again.
My God takes the broken
And makes them whole.

My God touched the outcast,
Raised the lame man,
And He caused the blind to see.
My God takes the broken
And makes them whole.

My God stood for justice,
Shamed the prideful,
But He called the sinner 'friend'.
My God takes the broken
And makes them whole.

My God felt the anguish
Of the soldier,
Made his child to live again.
My God takes the broken
And makes them whole.

My God, mocked and beaten,
Crushed and bleeding,
Yet crying, 'Father God, forgive.'
My God became broken
To make me whole.

My God, on the third day,
In the morning,
Broke the shackles of the grave.
My God took the broken
And made Him whole.

My God knows my failures,
Speaks forgiveness,
Gives me strength to try again.
My God takes the broken
And makes me whole.

1970

New music & adapt. of words by Frederick W. Faber (1814–1863)
Nick Herbert & Tom Eccleshall

MY GOD, HOW WONDERFUL YOU ARE,
Your majesty how bright;
How beautiful Your throne of grace
In depths of burning light.

How wonderful, how beautiful
The sight of You must be.
How wonderful, how beautiful,
Perfect purity.

(Second time)
My God, how wonderful You are.
My God, how wonderful You are.

No earthly father loves like You,
No mother half as mild;
Such loving kindness daily shown
To me, Your precious child.

Father of Jesus, love's great reward,
What rapture will it be
To kneel before Your throne in the heavens
And gaze and gaze on Thee?

1971

Andy Bromley

MY GREATEST SONG IS MY LIFE,
Poured out for You.
My greatest love,
Let it be seen in all I do.
My greatest hope, greatest joy,
Greatest peace is found in You.
Jesus, my passion is for You.

My greatest devotion
To love and to serve You;
My greatest desire
To live all my days
For my Saviour, my healer,
My friend and my God.
Jesus, to You;
My greatest devotion is to You.

1972

Stuart Townend & Keith Getty

MY HEART IS FILLED WITH THANKFULNESS
To Him who bore my pain;
Who plumbed the depths of my disgrace
And gave me life again;
Who crushed my curse of sinfulness
And clothed me with His light,
And wrote His law of righteousness
With power upon my heart.

My heart is filled with thankfulness
To Him who walks beside;
Who floods my weaknesses with strength
And causes fears to fly;
Whose every promise is enough
For every step I take,
Sustaining me with arms of love
And crowning me with grace.

My heart is filled with thankfulness
To Him who reigns above;
Whose wisdom is my perfect peace,
Whose every thought is love.
For every day I have on earth
Is given by the King.
So I will give my life, my all,
To love and follow Him.

1973

Reuben Morgan

MY SAVIOUR, REDEEMER,
Lifted me from the miry clay.
Almighty, forever,
I will never be the same,

'Cause You came near,
From the everlasting
To the world we live,
The Father's only Son.

And You lived and You died,
And You rose again on high,
And You opened the way
For the world to live again.
Hallelujah for all You've done.

1974

Aaron Keyes & Stuart Townend

MY SOUL FINDS REST in God alone,
My rock and my salvation;
A fortress strong against my foes,
And I will not be shaken.
Though lips may bless and hearts may curse,
And lies like arrows pierce me,
I'll fix my heart on righteousness,
I'll look to Him who hears me.

O praise Him, hallelujah,
My delight and my reward;
Everlasting, never failing,
My Redeemer, my God.

Find rest my soul in God alone
Amid the world's temptations;
When evil seeks to take a hold
I'll cling to my salvation.
Though riches come and riches go,
Don't set your heart upon them;
The fields of hope in which I sow
Are harvested in heaven.

I'll set my gaze on God alone
And trust in Him completely;
With every day pour out my soul
And He will prove His mercy.
Though life is but a fleeting breath,
A sigh too brief to measure,
My King has crushed the curse of death
And I am His forever.

1975

Tim Hughes & Martin Smith

MY SOUL IS WEAK, my heart is numb,
I cannot see,
But still my hope is found in You.
I hold on tightly,
You will never let me go,
For, Jesus, You will never fail,
Jesus, You will never fail.

Simply to the cross I cling;
Letting go of all earthly things,
I'm clinging to the cross.
Mercy's found a way for me,
Hope is here as I am free.
Jesus, You are all I need;
I'm clinging to the cross.

Even darkness is as light
To You, my Lord,
So light the way and lead me home
To that place where
Every tear is wiped away,
For, Jesus, You will never fail,
Jesus, You will never fail.

What a Saviour, what a story,
You were crucified, but now You are alive.
So amazing, such a mystery,
You were crucified, but now You are alive.

1976

Chris Bowater

NOT TO US, O LORD,
But to Your name be glory.
Not to us be praise,
But Your great name we raise.

High above, lifted up,
You deserve the place of honour.
Holy One, glorious Christ,
You deserve our heart's devotion.

Christ the King, heaven's Lamb,
Jesus, You alone are worthy
To receive the offering
Of forgiven hearts in worship.

Ransomed, healed, restored, forgiven,
Who like we His praise should sing?
Ransomed, healed, restored, forgiven,
Praise the everlasting King,
Praise the everlasting King.

1977

Keith & Kristyn Getty

NOW MAY THE FRAGRANCE of His peace
Soar through your heart like a dove released:
Hide in His wings, O weary, distant soul;
He'll guide your spirit home.

And may His love poured from on high
Flow to the depths of your deepest sigh;
Oh, come and drink from the only living stream,
And on His shoulder lean.

And may the hope that will not deceive
Through every pain bring eternal ease;
There is no night that can steal the promises
His coming brings to us.

So may His joy rush over you;
Delight in the path He has called you to;
May all your steps walk in heaven's endless light
*Beyond this Christmas night.

**Alternative last line:*
Make your sole purpose Christ.

1978

Martin Rinkart (1586–1649)
Tr. Catherine Winkworth (1827–1878)
Music and chorus: Ian Hannah

NOW THANK WE ALL OUR GOD,
With hearts and hands and voices;
Who wondrous things hath done,
In whom this world rejoices;
Who from our mother's arms
Hath blessed us on our way
With countless gifts of love,
And still is ours today.

Give thanks unto the Lord.
(Repeat)

O may this bounteous God
Through all our life be near us,
With ever joyful hearts
And blessèd peace to cheer us;

And keep us in His grace,
And guide us when perplexed,
And free us from all ills
In this world and the next.

All praise and thanks to God
The Father now be given;
The Son and Him who reigns
With them in highest heaven;
The one eternal God,
Whom earth and heaven adore;
For thus it was, is now,
And shall be evermore.

1979

Keith Getty & Phil Madeira

O BREATH OF GOD, come fill this place,
Revive our hearts to know Your grace,
And from our slumber make us rise,
That we may know the risen Christ.

O Word of God, so clear and true,
Renew our minds to trust in You,
And give to us the bread of life,
That we may know the risen Christ.

O Love of God, so unrestrained,
Refresh our souls in Jesus' name.
Let us reflect Your sacrifice,
That we may know the living Christ.

May God the Father, God the Son
And God the Spirit make us one;
In holiness let us unite,
That we may know the risen Christ.

1980 Charlie Hall & Matt Redman

O CHRIST, BE THE CENTRE *of our lives,*
Be the place we fix our eyes,
Be the centre of our lives.

And You're the centre of the universe –
Everything was made in You, Jesus.
Breath of every living thing,
Everyone was made for You.
You hold everything together.
You hold everything together.

We lift our eyes to heaven
And we wrap our lives around Your life.
We lift our eyes to heaven, to You.
(Repeat)

1981 Stuart Townend & Keith Getty

O CHURCH, ARISE and put your armour on;
Hear the call of Christ our Captain.
For now the weak can say that they are strong
In the strength that God has given.
With shield of faith and belt of truth,
We'll stand against the devil's lies;
An army bold, whose battle-cry is Love,
Reaching out to those in darkness.

Our call to war, to love the captive soul
But to rage against the captor;
And with the sword that makes the wounded whole,
We will fight with faith and valour.
When faced with trials on every side

We know the outcome is secure,
And Christ will have the prize for which He died,
An inheritance of nations.

Come see the cross, where love and mercy meet,
As the Son of God is stricken;
Then see His foes lie crushed beneath His feet,
For the Conqueror has risen!
And as the stone is rolled away,
And Christ emerges from the grave,
This victory march continues till the day
Every eye and heart shall see Him.

So Spirit, come, put strength in every stride,
Give grace for every hurdle,
That we may run with faith to win the prize
Of a servant good and faithful.
As saints of old still line the way,
Retelling triumphs of His grace,
We hear their calls, and hunger for the day
When with Christ we stand in glory.

1982

Gareth Robinson

O GOD, THE GOD OF BLESSING,
The God of kindness,
The God of open-hearted love.
God of grace and God of mercy,
God of earth and heaven above.
God and Father of our Lord Jesus Christ.

Glory to the Father,
Glory to the Son,
Glory to the Spirit,
The three in one.

You sent Your Son from glory
To be our Saviour,
To take on flesh and live like us.
Now heaven's open, forgiveness purchased
On the altar of the cross;
Now exalted as our Lord Jesus Christ.

He sent Your Holy Spirit
Straight from heaven,
Guaranteeing what's to come:
To be made whole and be made holy
In the kingdom of Your Son;
Giving glory to our Lord Jesus Christ.

There is none like You. *(x4)*

1983

Keith Getty & Margaret Becker

OH, FOR A HEART *to serve my God;*
A heart that's ever broken to His will.
Oh, for a heart to serve my God, my King;
A heart that's ever delighting Him.

Oh, that I would be made pure,
That I would strive to love Him more;
That every work of my hands
Would accomplish all His plans,
So that He would be glorified.

That I would place no other above;
That I would die to lift high my God.
That every blessing I enjoy
Would always be employed
In the service of my faithful Lord.

1984

Noel Robinson & Donna Akodu

OH, HE'S SO SWEET.
Oh, He's so sweet.

He's the reason why I sing,
He is my Lord and King;
That is why I bring this holy offering.
He's the lifter of my soul,
He cleansed and made me whole.
He's taken all my sadness
And filled me with His gladness.

Jehovah Jireh, my provider.
Jehovah Nissi, He's my banner.
Jehovah Raphi, He's my healer,
Sweeter than the honey
From the honeycomb.

1985

Charlie Hall

OH, MY HEART LONGS TO BE PURIFIED;
Oh, my heart longs to be refined.

A holy heart is what I long for,
What I cry for, what I need;
A heart that loves You,
A heart that hears You, fears You,
And sees You as You are.

Search my heart, O God, and see in me
All offences, God, that there may be . . .

Refined in Your love, refined by Your blood.
And the pure in heart will see You,
Will see You.
We're cryin' out.

1986

Mark Beswick & Howard Francis

O HOLY SPIRIT,
We welcome You today.
Fill us with Your presence
As we give You the praise.
Lord, we are Your temple;
For You alone we wait.

Holy Spirit, welcome in this place.
Holy Spirit, come and take Your place.

We welcome You,
We welcome You.
Father, we welcome You.
(Repeat)

1987

David Gate

OH, THE BLOOD THAT FLOWED,
Oh, the crimson tide,
Where the sinless Saviour died
On the killing hill.

See His hands and feet,
Hear the painful cry,
See the darkened sky
On the killing hill.

Love without measure,
Love without bounds;
Love that lasts forever
On the killing hill.

Where the will of God was met,
Eternal justice sealed,
Mercy was revealed
On the killing hill.

1988 Keith Getty & Stuart Townend

OH, TO SEE THE DAWN
Of the darkest day:
Christ on the road to Calvary.
Tried by sinful men,
Torn and beaten then
Nailed to a cross of wood.

This, the power of the cross:
Christ became sin for us.
Took the blame, bore the wrath –
We stand forgiven at the cross.

Oh, to see the pain
Written on Your face,
Bearing the awesome weight of sin.
Every bitter thought,
Every evil deed
Crowning Your bloodstained brow.

Now the daylight flees,
Now the ground beneath
Quakes as its maker bows His head.
Curtain torn in two,
Dead are raised to life;
'Finished!' the victory cry.

Oh, to see my name
Written in the wounds,
For through Your suffering I am free.
Death is crushed to death,
Life is mine to live,
Won through Your selfless love.

(Final chorus)
This, the power of the cross:
Son of God – slain for us.
What a love! What a cost!
We stand forgiven at the cross.

1989

Mark Tedder, John Hartley & Tom Lane

OH, WHAT POWER, oh, what strength,
That a King would come into my life.
Oh, what kindness, oh, what peace,
As a crown of thorns displays Your majesty.
Bearing pain, just a man, but a man
For whom the world's not worthy.

Stars screaming such splendour,
All of heaven's beauty,
Shining with the glory of the Lord.
Revealing such wonder,
All of His creation
Caught up in the mystery of God.

Burning passion for the world;
Out of love He became the sin for us.
Sovereign King, chosen One,
Perfect Lamb, a Lamb so undeserving.
In Your pain, just a man, but a man
For whom the world's not worthy.

1990

Nick Herbert & John Peters

O LORD, MAY I DWELL in Your sanctuary?
O Lord, may I stand in Your glory?
By Your matchless mercy.
By Your matchless mercy.

O Lord, may I see Your majesty?
O Lord, may I taste Your purity?
By Your matchless mercy.
By Your matchless mercy.

1991

Lara Martin (Abundant Life Ministries, Bradford, England)

O LORD, YOU ARE MY KEEPER,
I will never be in want;
You hold me close, so tender,
And quiet me with love.
And I hear You singing over me,
I hear You singing over me.

Songs of countless promises,
Like kisses from heaven they fall:
'How loved am I!'
Songs that take me to higher heights,
Such favour I know is divine:
'How loved am I, how loved am I!'

O Lord, You are my keeper,
My heart is safe with You.
Though in life there will be valleys,
You take my hand and lead me through.

1992

Paul Oakley

ON A DARK NIGHT shone a star bright
Over sleepy Bethlehem.
Skies were ringing, angels singing,
Peace on earth, goodwill to men.

See the baby in the manger,
Born to save us from our sin.
Hallelujah! What a Saviour!
This is Jesus Christ the King.

Shepherds hasten to the stable
Where the holy infant lay,
As the wise men from the East bring
Precious gifts to Mary's babe.

Can this baby in the manger
Really save us from our sin?
Hallelujah! What a Saviour!
This is Jesus Christ the King.

Soon it will be Christmas morning,
Cards and gifts around the tree;
But will you treasure, will you worship
Jesus born to set us free?

And this baby in the manger
Died to save us from our sin.
Hallelujah! What a Saviour!
Jesus Christ the King of kings.

1993

Dave Bilbrough

ONE HEART, ONE SPIRIT;
We are called by God
To reach out and serve one another
In the Father's love.

We've started a journey
And the road may be long;
We won't be distracted
Till the work is all done.
We'll follow His leading,
We'll do what He asks,
'Cause we're moving forward,
Not back to the past.

The way may be costly,
The price will be great;
We're going the distance
Whatever it takes.
It won't be easy,

There'll be times we're confused;
But when we stand together
His love will shine through.

We are marching to the sound
Of a different drum.
(Repeat)

1994 Andy Bromley

ONE THING I HAVE DESIRED of You, Lord;
That will I seek:
To dwell in Your house forever more,
To behold Your beauty,
At Your feet adore You.

Such beauty,
No words can describe You;
You are lovely,
Beautiful Son of God.
Such beauty
Leaves me speechless,
Leaves me speechless.

1995 Matt Redman

ONE THING MY HEART IS SET UPON,
One thing that I would ask:
To know You, Lord, as close as one
Could hope to on this earth.

Intimacy, O Jesus, intimacy.
My treasure will be, O Jesus,
Your intimacy.

To look upon Your beauty, Lord,
Your glory and Your heart;
To know You close and closer still
Each day upon this earth.

Lord, since the day I saw You first,
My soul was satisfied;
And yet because I see in part,
I'm searching more to find.

1996

Martyn Layzell, Nathan Fellingham & busbee

ON HOLY GROUND we stand before
The King of kings and Lord of all,
Where saints have walked this road before,
Carried their cross through heaven's door.
To the King of heaven all the angels sing.

And I will join the song,
An ancient melody;
A song that I will sing
For all eternity.
It's all around the world,
Hearts in harmony,
Worship to the King
Who reigns eternally.
And I will join the song and sing.

(To repeat chorus)
Worship to the King of kings.
And I will join the song . . .

Awake, O church, lift up your eyes,
Let your light shine for all mankind.
Holding the flame of truth and life,
One heart, one voice, now unified.
To the King of heaven all creation sings.

1997

Paul & Lex Buckley

ON THAT DAY my pain will cease,
My heart will be healed,
My tears wiped away.
And You will be my peace,
You will be my peace.

On that day I will be home
And I'll rest in Your arms,
In my Father's arms.
And You will be my peace,
You will be my peace.

I will be home
I will be home.

1998

Graham Kendrick

ON THE BLOODSTAINED GROUND,
Where the shadow falls,
Of a cross and a crown of thorns,
I kneel down, I kneel down.
I lift my eyes to a tear-stained face;
Who is this dying in my place?
I kneel down, I kneel down.

I come just as I am,
This is my only plea,
One hope in which I trust,
This blood was shed for me.

As You wash the stains of my guilty heart,
Till I'm clean in every part,
I kneel down, I kneel down.
Wash away my shame, my pain, my pride,
Every sin that I once denied;
I kneel down, I kneel down.

This is where I'll always come,
This is where I'll always run,
To worship You.
This is where I'll always come,
This is where I'll always run,
To worship You.

(Last time)
To worship You, Jesus.
Jesus, worship Jesus.
Jesus, worship Jesus.

1999

Tré Sheppard

ON THE SHORES OF OUR DOUBT,
On the sands of our pain,
We found a river of grace
And it flows with Your hope.
We come to the stream;
Wash us in the river again.

From the darkest place, the deepest pain,
Where the tears fall down like rain,
We will call to You:
'Your kingdom come,
Your will be done again.'
When we can't find You or see Your face,
When we've used up all our faith,
Will You rescue us from ourselves,
And carry us to grace?

You are the One who understands,
You lived down here, became a man,
So we could hope again.
Now take us to the river wide;
From these ashes we will rise,
Our brokenness undone.

How can it be we found such love? *(x3)*
Won't you come to the river?
Oh, come down and find grace.
(Repeat)

2000

Neil Bennetts

O PERFECT LOVE, O perfect sacrifice,
Fountain of life poured out for me.
What heights and depths of heaven's mercy,
The faithfulness that I believe.
And to whom shall I run?
And in whom shall I hide?
Only You hold the truth I desire.
O perfect love, my prayer shall ever be
To be found in Jesus.

O perfect love, O perfect mystery,
You were condemned, but I go free.
What truth to know that I can rest upon:
Your perfect love has covered me.
And what can this heart know,
And what can this heart tell,
But of grace that has rescued me?
O perfect love,
My prayer shall ever be
To be found in Jesus.

O perfect love, forever I shall sing
Of heaven's gates flung wide for me,
Where fear of death and tears of hopelessness
Are swallowed up in victory.
And what praise shall be sung
Still to the holy One;
To the Saviour, Redeemer and King.
O perfect love,
My song will ever be:
'I am found in Jesus.'

2001 Vicky Beeching

O PRECIOUS SIGHT, my Saviour stands,
Dying for me with outstretched hands.
O precious sight; I love to gaze,
Remembering salvation day,
Remembering salvation day.

Though my eyes linger on this scene,
May passing time and years not steal
The power with which it impacts me,
The freshness of its mystery,
The freshness of its mystery.

May I never lose the wonder,
The wonder of the cross.
May I see it like the first time,
Standing as a sinner lost.
Undone by mercy and left speechless,
Watching wide-eyed at the cost.
May I never lose the wonder,
The wonder of the cross.

Behold, the God–Man crucified,
The perfect sinless sacrifice.
As blood ran down those nails and wood,
History was split in two,
History was split in two.

Behold, the empty wooden tree,
His body gone, alive and free.
We sing with everlasting joy,
For sin and death have been destroyed,
Sin and death have been destroyed.

2002

Chris Bowater & David Lyon

O THE DEEP, DEEP LOVE *of Jesus,*
Vast, unmeasured, boundless, free,
Rolling like the mighty ocean
In its fullness over me;
O the deep, deep love.
(Repeat)

Ancient hope now born to man,
Faithful through all time.
Crucified yet raised to life,
O the deep, deep love.

Constant in a changing world,
Healer of our pain.
Comfort to the grieving soul,
O the deep, deep love.

Giver of eternal days,
When this life will end.
At His feet to lay our crowns,
O the deep, deep love.

2003

Words: S.T. Francis (1834–1925)
Music: Ian Hannah

O THE DEEP, DEEP LOVE OF JESUS!
Vast, unmeasured, boundless, free;
Rolling as a mighty ocean
In its fullness over me.
Underneath me, all around me,
Is the current of Thy love;
Leading onward, leading homeward,
To my glorious rest above.
O the deep, deep love,

Vast, unmeasured, boundless, free.
O the deep, deep love,
In its fullness over me.

O the deep, deep love of Jesus!
Spread His praise from shore to shore,
How He loveth, ever loveth,
Changeth never, never more;
How He watches o'er His loved ones,
Died to call them all His own.
How for them He intercedeth,
Watcheth o'er them from the throne.
O the deep, deep love,
Spread His praise from shore to shore.
O the deep, deep love,
Changeth never, never more.

O the deep, deep love of Jesus!
Love of every love the best:
'Tis an ocean vast of blessing,
'Tis a haven sweet of rest.
O the deep, deep love of Jesus!
'Tis a heaven of heavens to me;
And it lifts me up to glory,
For it lifts me up to Thee.
O the deep, deep love,
Love of every love the best.
O the deep, deep love,
'Tis a haven sweet of rest.

2004

Jo & Nigel Hemming

OUR GOD IS A GREAT BIG GOD,
Our God is a great big God,
Our God is a great big God
And He holds us in His hands.

He's higher than a skyscraper
And He's deeper than a submarine.
He's wider than the universe
And beyond my wildest dreams.
And He's known me and He's loved me
Since before the world began.
How wonderful to be a part
Of God's amazing plan!

2005

Lowell Alexander, Keith Getty & Joanne Hogg

OVER FIELDS OF GREEN from north and south,
Across the sea of blue,
Let the joy of such creative power
Release our song to You.

United by Your promise
So faithful and so true,
As Your Spirit soars within our hearts,
Our song shall rise to You,
Our song shall rise to You.

So may the music of our song
Release a healing power,
And with all God's angels join our hearts
In heaven's song above.

2006

Matt Redman

PRAISE AWAITS YOU IN THIS PLACE TODAY, O Lord.
We are gathered, ready, God, to sing Your praise.
Ready to respond
To the glories of Your name,
To the wonders of Your heart,
To Your great love.

Praise is waiting for You in this place;
There's a cry that our spirits will make
As we see Your glory.
To Your mercies our souls will awake,
And we'll sing till the break of the day,
Because You are worthy.

Seasons come and seasons go, but You remain,
So unchanging, all-deserving of our praise.
Ready to respond
To the glories of Your name,
To the wonders of Your heart,
To Your great love.

2007

Brenton Brown & Paul Baloche

PRAISE IS RISING, eyes are turning to You,
We turn to You.
Hope is stirring, hearts are yearning for You,
We long for You.

'Cause when we see You,
We find strength to face the day;
In Your presence
All our fears are washed away,
Washed away.

Hosanna, hosanna,
You are the God who saves us,
Worthy of all our praises.
Hosanna, hosanna,
Come, have Your way among us;
We welcome You here, Lord Jesus.

Hear the sound of hearts returning to You,
We turn to You.
In Your kingdom broken lives are made new,
You make all things new.

2008 Paul Oakley

PRAISES TO THE HOLY ONE
For the wonders You have done.
Praise in every tribe and tongue,
Jesus, to You be sung.

Let every voice, let every song,
Let every instrument and sound,
Declare the wonders of our God.
Let all Your holy ones proclaim
The glory of our Saviour's name.
Let all the earth resound with praise,
Jesus, to You.

Praise Him for His mighty power,
Sun and moon and stars bow down.
Praise in all creation now,
Jesus, to You resounds.

Angels help us to adore
As we bow our hearts in awe.
Praise and honour evermore,
Jesus, to You our Lord.

Let everything that lives and breathes,
Let every mountain, every sea,
Reflect the beauty of our God.
Let every heart burst into song,
Let every word upon my tongue
Declare the praise of who You are.

2009

Charlie Hall, Kendall Combes, Brian Bergman, Will Hunt & Todd Cromwell

PRAISE THE FATHER, who
From heaven came to me;
By the Saviour,
In His mercy set me free.

Yeah, I run like the river,
Dance like the summer.
Joy is in my heart;
You have satisfied my soul.
Yeah, I run like the river,
Dance like the summer.
Joy is in my heart;
You have satisfied.

Praise His name, praise His name,
All the earth celebrate.
Praise His name, praise His name,
All the earth.

2010

Godfrey Birtill

PURIFY MY IMAGINATION
With Your beauty, O Lord.
Nourish my mind with Your truth,
That I may worship.
Quicken my conscience to Your holiness
In Your presence, O Lord.
Open my heart to Your love,
That I may worship.

Sweet adoration, sweet adoration.
Holy, holy, holy is the Lord.
(Repeat)

Take away the sting of bitterness
By Your mercy, O Lord.
Awaken my soul to Your grace,
That I may worship.
How can I hold unforgiveness,
Knowing You forgive me?
I surrender my life, my all,
That I may worship.

2011

Paul Oakley

RAISE A BANNER, raise it up high,
To every people under the sky;
Prepare the way for them to come in.
Build a highway, open the gates,
Remove the stones that stand in the way;
Humble your hearts and turn from every sin.
All you watchmen, lift up your cry
Through the day and into the night.
The Lord on whom you call
Will surely come.

We are His bride,
We are His people;
A crown in the hand of the Lord,
His true delight.
We are the light,
A city on a hill:
So hold out this word of hope
And let your light shine.
We are the light.

For Zion's sake I will not rest.
I will restore Jerusalem
Until she shines like the morning sun.
And then all kings will see her glory,
A blazing torch, pure and holy,

Her new name, 'The praise of all the earth'.
No more ignored, no longer despised,
He won't forsake His precious bride.
The Lord has given His word
And He does not lie.

2012

Shaun Griffiths

RIGHTEOUS, HOLY, WORTHY ARE YOU.
Amazing power, worthy are You.
One day every knee will bow
And every tongue confess
That You are the only One
That's worthy of our praise.

You are the living God,
Righteous and holy and powerful.
You are the only God.
You are the way, the truth, the life,
You are.

2013

Jonas Myrin & Marty Sampson

SAVED BY YOUR MERCY,
Found in Your grace,
Totally surrendered to Your embrace,
And there's nothing more than You.
See Your perfection,
I'm lost in Your peace;
Your faithfulness sings over me,
And Your love is the light of my soul.

And I lift my eyes to You,
Creator of the world.

And I stand in awe of You,
Of Your glory.
And I live to worship You,
Son of God, King of heaven.
And the angels round Your throne
Cry out 'holy'
To the One who is to come.
Hear us sing, 'Hallelujah.'

Hallelujah, hallelujah,
Hallelujah.
(Repeat)

2014

Mark Tedder & Paul Oakley

SAVIOUR, CLOSER THAN A BROTHER,
There could be no other like You.
Keep me closer to the fire,
Filled with strong desire for You.

And I'll stay on pilgrim's journey,
Knowing You're with me,
Comforting God.

You are good in all that You do,
Covenant-keeping God;
You are faithful and true.
And I'll stand strong in Your grace,
Trusting Your word, O God,
And through all things
Your love will endure.

Take me deeper than the healing,
Further than the grieving, Jesus.
Wake me, make me more than ever
Hungry for Your presence, First Love.

Lead me deeper in Your river;
Fill me with Your power, Spirit.
Change me, shape me in Your image
As You intervene in my life.

2015

Kate Simmonds & Mark Edwards

SAVIOUR, I MUST SING
Of love that bore my sin for me;
Freely welcomed in,
With gifts of life and liberty.
You let me rise with dignity,
And turn my shame into a shout of praise.

Jesus, sacrifice of God,
Hope of every heart,
Saviour of the world.
Jesus! Behold the Son of man,
The Lord, the great I Am,
Saviour of the world.

I have seen the King,
Crowned with power and majesty.
My hope is set on Him
Who reigns with all authority.
Now saved for all eternity,
Let all who know His mercy give Him praise.

Your blood was shed;
The wrath of God is turned away.
Eternal life for all who call upon Your name.
And multitudes will bow before Your throne and praise.
Your righteousness brings many sons to glory.
(Repeat)
Glory, glory.

2016

Vicky Beeching

SEARCH ME, O GOD;
Search me and find
Any way in me
That does not reflect Your purity.
Refine me, O God,
In the fire of Your gaze,
That I might be holy in all of my ways.
Take me deeper, Lord.
Draw me closer, Lord.

Give me a heart
After Your own heart.
Give me a mind that is pure
And pleasing to You.
Fill me with love,
With Your power and Your joy,
That this world might see You in me.

2017

Tom Lockley

SEE HIS LOVE nailed to a cross,
Perfect and blameless life given as sacrifice.
See Him there, all in the name of love,
Broken yet glorious, all for the sake of us.

This is Jesus in His glory,
King of heaven, dying for me.
It is finished, He has done it.
Death is beaten, heaven beckons me.

Greater love no one could ever show,
Mercy so undeserved, freedom I should not know.
All my sin, all of my hidden shame,
Died with Him on the cross, eternity won for us.

Such love, such love,
Such love is this for me.
(Repeat)

2018

Robert Critchley

SEEMS LIKE SO LONG AGO,
Upon a rugged cross,
Jesus, the Lamb of God,
Was crucified for us.
The ransom there was paid
To set the sinner free,
And His blood still cries mercy over me.

> *Still cries mercy, mercy, mercy.*
> *His blood still cries mercy over me.*
> (Repeat)

My Saviour's dying words
Expressed love pure and true:
'Father, forgive them,
For they know not what they do.'
He interceded there
Despite His agony,
And His prayer still pleads mercy over me.

> *Still pleads mercy, mercy, mercy.*
> *His prayer still pleads mercy over me.*
> (Repeat)

I thank You, Lord,
That I don't get what I deserve;
I thank You for Your awesome grace.
Instead of judgement,
The abundance of Your love,
Goodness and mercy all my days.

2019

Chris Tomlin, Ed Cash & Jesse Reeves

SEE THE MORNING, see it rising
Over the mountains high.
See the mercy in the mighty hand of God.
Living water, come and fill us;
Only You can satisfy.
Turn our sorrow into singing
The song of life.

Rejoice, rejoice,
And sing with the angel voices.
Rejoice, rejoice,
All heaven and earth rejoice.

Lord, Your strength is a tower
The righteous run into.
Lord, Your love is a banner over us.
And we hold on to the promise
That Your hold on us is true.
There's no other like You, Jesus,
No one like You.

Always,
Again I say rejoice.

2020

Stuart Townend & Keith Getty

SEE, WHAT A MORNING, gloriously bright,
With the dawning of hope in Jerusalem;
Folded, the grave-clothes,
Tomb filled with light,
As the angels announce Christ is risen!
See God's salvation plan,

Wrought in love, borne in pain,
Paid in sacrifice,
Fulfilled in Christ the Man,
For He lives, Christ is risen from the dead!

See Mary weeping, 'Where is He laid?'
As in sorrow she turns from the empty tomb;
Hears a voice speaking,
Calling her name;
It's the Master, the Lord raised to life again!
The voice that spans the years,
Speaking life, stirring hope,
Bringing peace to us,
Will sound till He appears,
For He lives, Christ is risen from the dead!

One with the Father, Ancient of Days,
Through the Spirit who clothes faith with certainty;
Honour and blessing,
Glory and praise
To the King crowned with power and authority!
And we are raised with Him,
Death is dead, love has won,
Christ has conquered;
And we shall reign with Him,
For He lives, Christ is risen from the dead!

2021

Paul Oakley

SHEPHERD OF MY THANKFUL HEART,
Ever-faithful friend You are;
Healer who now bears the scars
Of love's amazing grace.

Heaven's song made flesh for us,
Crucified upon the cross;
Now in glory, Jesus,
To You belongs all praise.

Be glorified in me.
Be glorified in me.
Be glorified in me,
Jesus, my King.

Sacrifice no words could tell,
Majesty on earth to dwell;
Living Word, Emmanuel,
I'll love You all my days.

Maker of the stars above,
Praise of angels ever sung;
King of glory, King of love,
Let all creation praise.

2022

Sammy Horner, John Hartley & Phil Madeira

SHOW MERCY, *act wisely,*
Live justly before Your God.
Love loyally, unfailingly,
Consistently before Your God.

This is our destiny, our hope for unity,
Our servant hearts should be mirrors of God.
And live accordingly,
So that this world may see
God's love so beautifully
In each of our lives.

This is our destiny, to follow faithfully,
Give as He gave for free
And lay down our lives,
And so reflect His light.
His truth can't be denied
If we will love like Christ and honour our God.

2023

Chris Bowater

SHOW ME YOUR WAYS,
Show me now Your glory.
I want to know You more.
Show me Your ways,
Show me now Your glory.
I want to know You more.

In the stillness,
I settle my heart in silence,
Patiently waiting for You,
Adoring You.
In these moments,
Touched by the hand of mercy,
Drawn by transforming beauty,
I worship You.

Gracious God, compassionate Lord,
Slow to wrath, abounding in love.
Gracious God, compassionate Lord,
Slow to wrath, abounding in love.
Adoring You, I worship You,
Standing in awe of You.

2024

Billy James Foote
1st verse and theme from 'Sing we the King'
by Charles Silvester Horne (1865–1914)

SING TO THE KING who is coming to reign;
Glory to Jesus, the Lamb that was slain.
Life and salvation His empire shall bring,
And joy to the nations when Jesus is King.

Come, let us sing a song,
A song declaring that we belong to Jesus;
He is all we need.

Lift up a heart of praise,
Sing now with voices raised to Jesus:
Sing to the King.

For His returning we watch and we pray;
We will be ready the dawn of that day.
We'll join in singing with all the redeemed,
'Cause Satan is vanquished and Jesus is King.

2025

Nathan & Lou Fellingham & busbee

SING TO THE LORD,
Give thanks for His greatness.
Sing to the Lord,
Give thanks for His grace.
His mercy is new today,
Abounding in every way
To all He has made.

Sing to the Lord,
Give thanks for His favour.
Sing to the Lord,
O people of God.
We're so precious in His sight,
He chose us before our life
Even began.

Lift up your voice
And tell of His goodness,
For He is perfect in all of His ways.
Join in the song
That is sung over all of the earth:
Lord, You're an amazing God.

Sing to the Lord,
Give thanks for salvation.
Sing to the Lord,

All you who are saved,
For once we were dead in sin,
But now we're alive in Him,
And reigning with Christ.

Sing, sing, sing, sing!
(Repeat)

Sing to the Lord,
Give thanks for His kindness.
Sing to the Lord,
O children of God.
The Spirit's available,
He'll help us prevail through all
That life throws our way.

Sing to the Lord,
Give thanks for His power.
Sing to the Lord,
His kingdom is here.
Let's humble our hearts to Him,
Be ready to meet Him
As we call on His name.

2026

Andy Ferret & Marc James

SING TO THE LORD, FOR HE IS GOOD.
Give thanks to Him,
Tell all the world of all He's done.
Come lift your voice to worship Him,
Come shout aloud.
Open up, you gates, you ancient doors,
Let His glory in.

Hallelujah, King forever,
All the earth will bow.
God most holy, You're so worthy,
We will praise You now.

He is a God of favour, mercy and grace;
He reaches out with arms held wide.
Who is this King of glory?
He's Lord of all.
Open up, you gates, you ancient doors,
Let His glory in.

Let the heavens rejoice, let the earth be glad,
Let the seas resound with praise.
Let us join as one with creation's song,
Lifting up a sound of praise.

2027

Mark Beswick, Howard Francis & Nicky Brown

SING UNTO THE LORD A NEW SONG.
Bless Him, praise Him,
Lift Him higher.
All you chosen generation,
Dance and celebrate.
(Repeat)

If you lift Him high,
He will draw us nearer,
Ever closer to Him
Day by day.
If you lift Him high,
He will draw us nearer,
Ever closer to Him
Every day.

2028

Matt & Beth Redman

SO FEARFULLY AND WONDERFULLY MADE,
How could they say there is no God?
Reminded every breath that I take,
It's by Your hand I have been formed.

So what am I going to do
With this life You gave me?
What could I do but live for Your praise?

You gave me this breath
And You gave me this strength,
And every day I'll live to obey You.
With all of my heart,
With all of my soul,
Let every breath I'm breathing display You, God.

There's elegance in all You create,
Your grand designs leave me amazed.
The wonders of the way we've been made
Speak of Your power, tell of Your grace.

So what am I going to do
With this life You gave me?
What am I going to do with this life?
What am I going to do
In these days You've ordained?
What am I going to do with this life?

2029

Brenton Brown & Daniel Ornellas
Chorus: H. G. Spafford (1828–1888) & P. Bliss (1838–1876)

SOMETIMES IT'S HARD, sometimes I cry,
Sometimes my heart wants to know why.
But Your yoke is easy and Your burden is light;
And though my heart is aching
And there are tears in my eyes:

Whatever my lot,
You have taught me to know
It is well, it is well with my soul.

It's not always easy, I'm not always right;
Sometimes I do things that are wrong in Your sight.
But I have decided I'm gonna follow Jesus;
There's no turning back,
There's no turning back.

'Cause You have reached down to me,
You have rescued me,
You have shed Your blood for my soul.
And I live now knowing that the sky
And not the grave will be my goal.
And just as in life, also in death,
This truth will comfort and console:
That soon I will see Your face and hear Your voice
And know that it is well.

But please hold my hand, Lord,
And hold on tight,
'Cause the road here is narrow,
The road here is narrow.

2030

Brenton Brown

SO MUCH LOVE, so much light,
I'm alive again,
My first breath gazing into You.
Open eyes, I can see
You've been calling me;
This is who I was meant to be.

And I'm so alive, so alive,
Living in this love divine.
I'm so amazed, so amazed at You.
Moved from dark to blazing light,
Your love took me by surprise.
Now I never want to live away from You.
I don't ever want to live away from You.

Breathing out, breathing in,
I'm revived in Your love.
So content, so dependent on You.
Just a child, but I'm Yours,
What a mystery that You,
The God of all, would make me Your own.

So alive, so alive,
I'm living in this love,
Living in this love divine.
You changed my life, You saved my life,
You put Your love so deep inside.
You turned things round, You set things right,
I'm dancing in this love I've found.

2031

Vicky Beeching

SON OF GOD, You reign in heaven's glory,
Yet You chose to come to earth and save me.
Humbled Yourself to die the cruellest death;
No other act of love compares to this.

The greatest gift I've ever received
Is the cross, the cross.
For there You gave Yourself up for me
On the cross, the cross.
And with the blood You poured out for me,
You have saved my soul.
You have given me the greatest gift of all.

Your heart aches for all the lost and hurting.
At the cross You wait to take our burdens,
Longing to heal our wounds and make us whole;
Longing to hear us sing with thankful souls.

2032

Keith Getty & Stuart Townend

SPEAK, O LORD, as we come to You
To receive the food of Your holy word.
Take Your truth, plant it deep in us;
Shape and fashion us in Your likeness,
That the light of Christ might be seen today
In our acts of love and our deeds of faith.
Speak, O Lord, and fulfil in us
All Your purposes, for Your glory.

Teach us, Lord, full obedience,
Holy reverence, true humility.
Test our thoughts and our attitudes
In the radiance of Your purity.
Cause our faith to rise, cause our eyes to see
Your majestic love and authority.
Words of power that can never fail;
Let their truth prevail over unbelief.

Speak, O Lord, and renew our minds;
Help us grasp the heights of Your plans for us.
Truths unchanged from the dawn of time
That will echo down through eternity.
And by grace we'll stand on Your promises,
And by faith we'll walk as You walk with us.
Speak, O Lord, till Your church is built
And the earth is filled with Your glory.

2033

Reuben Morgan

STAND BY EVERYTHING YOU SAID.
Stand by the promises we made.
Let go of everything I've done.
I'll run into Your open arms,
And all I know.

I love You more than life.
I love You more than life.

Fall back on everything You've done.
Fall back on everlasting arms.
When all the world is swept away,
You are the things I need.
You're the air I breathe.

How can it be You were the One
On the cross,
Lifted for all our shame?
How can it be the scars in Your hands
Are for me?
You are the King of all.

2034

Brenton Brown & Ken Riley

STRENGTH WILL RISE as we wait upon the Lord.
We will wait upon the Lord,
We will wait upon the Lord.
(Repeat)

Our God, You reign forever;
Our hope, our strong deliverer.

You are the everlasting God,
The everlasting God.
You do not faint, You won't grow weary.
You're the defender of the weak,
You comfort those in need.
You lift us up on wings like eagles.

2035

David Lyon

SURELY THE LORD IS IN THIS PLACE,
And now in His presence we wait,
Knowing that He has heard our cry
And He has come among us.

He is the King of wonder,
He is beyond compare.
He is creation's healer;
Who could ever share His glory?
He is our help in trouble,
He is our only strength.
He is the first and last,
Beginning and the end.

Surely the Lord is rich in love,
And now in His goodness we trust,
Knowing that He has seen our need
And He has come among us.

2036

Kendall Combes, Todd Cromwell & Charlie Hall

SWEET FORGIVENESS, my redemption;
You're a Saviour once for all and today.
Oh, the mercy, it comes to flood me.
Jesus, on the cross You took my place.

And I'm chasing after You,
'Cause You first chased after me.
And You purchased me with blood;
I am free, I am complete.
Now a child of my King,

Leaving old, I am made new.
'Cause You first chased after me,
I am chasing after You.

And I found my love, I found my love,
And my heart is dancing.
I found my love, I found my love,
And my heart is dancing, yeah.

2037

Frances R. Havergal (1836–1879)
Adpt. & new music Paul Oakley

TAKE MY LIFE AND LET IT BE
Consecrated, Lord, to Thee.
Take my moments and my days,
Let them flow in ceaseless praise.
Take my hands and let them move
At the impulse of Your love.
Take my feet and let them be
Swift and beautiful for Thee.

Oh, take my life, let it be
Consecrated, Lord, to Thee.
Oh, take my moments and my days,
Let them flow in ceaseless praise.

Take my voice and let me sing
Always only for my King.
Take my lips and let them speak
Of the love that set me free.
Take my silver and my gold,
Not a mite would I withhold.
Take my intellect and use
Every gift as You shall choose.

Take my will and let it bow,
You alone shall wear the crown.
Take my heart, make it Your own,

Let it be Your royal throne.
Take my love, my Lord, I pour
At Your feet its treasure store.
Take myself and I will be
Ever, only, all for Thee.

2038

Sammy Horner & John Hartley

TAKE THIS BREAD, *break it up;*
Take this wine, fill your cup;
It's My body, it's My blood shed for you.

Lamb of God, my heart will thank You:
Prince of Peace, my refuge be.
In my weakness, I will praise You,
As healing streams wash over me,
Healing streams wash over me.

Lamb of God, in times of trouble,
I will gladly turn to Thee.
In my pain, O Man of Sorrows,
Healing streams wash over me,
Healing streams wash over me.

2039

Chris Bowater

TEACH ME HOW TO PRAY, *Jesus.*
Teach me how to pray;
To touch Your throne,
Bring heaven down,
To release Your power.
Teach me how to pray, Jesus.
Teach me how to pray;
To touch Your heart,
To have faith that can mountains move.
Teach me how to pray.

Teach me the wonders of the secret place.
Teach me how I can even seek Your face.
Teach me to stand before the throne of grace.
Teach me how to pray.

Teach me how wholeness comes in brokenness.
Teach me how fullness comes in emptiness.
Teach me the higher ways of holiness.
Teach me how to pray.

2040

Gareth Robinson

THANK YOU, FATHER, for Your love for me. *(x3)*
And I love You,
I love You.

Thank you, Jesus, that You died for me. *(x3)*
And I love You,
I love You.

Thank you, Spirit, that You're here with me. *(x3)*
And I love You,
I love You.

2041

Simon Brading

THE BATTLE OF FAITH must go on;
Keep us from just singing songs.
Help us to stand and believe You;
Teach us to fight and press on.
The battle is already won;
The devil has been overthrown!
So if my God is for me,
Who shall I fear? I shall not fear.

By faith we will believe
In every promise that You give.
By faith, Jesus, we'll live,
Standing on all that You've said.
We're trusting in You, Lord.

Help us be strong in Your might,
Living by faith not by sight,
Not basing our faith on our feelings,
But stand on Your word in our lives.
Give us an attitude for war,
To fight for Your kingdom, O God;
For if my God is for me,
Who shall I fear? I shall not fear.

We will fight to the end,
We will fight to the end,
Never letting go of Your promises.
We will fight to the end,
We will fight to the end,
Never letting go of You.
(Repeat)

2042

Vicky Beeching

THE BLAZING SUNRISE, the endless oceans,
The spinning planets all reveal their maker's power.
They shout His glory, they shine His beauty,
Their voices cry an invitation to us all.
They are summoning every soul,
Summoning every soul.

This is a call to worship;
Let it echo all around the earth.
This is a call to bow down,
Give God the glory He deserves.

We have gathered to praise our maker,
We've come to worship Him,
For we have heard the call.
Let every nation and all creation
Join us worshipping the holy God of all,
As we cry out to all of this world,
Cry out to all of this world.

To the north and the south
Let this invitation resonate.
To the east and the west
Let this invitation resonate.
Till the north and the south,
Till the east and the west,
Overflow with praise.

2043

Nick Herbert & John Peters

THE DAY WILL COME when this world You've made
Will surely pass away.
I'll be blameless on that day.
In that dark hour Your act of love
Took my guilt away.
I'll be blameless on that day.

I will stand before the Lord
While saints and angels sing.
Lost in wonder, lifted up,
I'll glorify the King.
Free for all eternity,
The past now has no hold on me.
Thank You for this word of grace You say:
I'll be blameless on that day.

'It is finished!' was the cry
That took my shame away.
I'll be blameless on that day.

The gift of life You gave to me
Took Your life away.
I'll be blameless on that day.

2044

Matt Redman

THE DISEASE OF MY SOUL was spreading,
Eating me up on the inside,
Keeping my heart from Your new life.
And I see now where I was headed,
For there is no cure that can save us
Outside of Your mercy, Lord Jesus.

Yes, You stepped in with Your power to save,
Let forgiveness reign, worked a miracle within.

Thank You for healing me.
I was dying beneath my shame,
But You brought me to life again,
And I will sing:
Thank You for freeing me.
I was dead to the truth of You,
But my healing was in Your wounds,
And now I sing:
Thank You for healing me.

Though outwardly I may waste away,
On the inside I'll be more alive every day.
As I walk through times of pain and grief,
There's a deeper truth inside of me.
You have placed Your life inside of me, so I sing:

I'm alive, I'm alive,
I'm alive, I'm alive in You.
Thank You for healing me.
(Repeat)

2045

Evan Rogers

THE GREATEST DAY in all of life
Is not right now but years gone by,
When Jesus came into the world.
Our lives were bought at a great price
When You became our sacrifice
And bore God's wrath for our offence.

And when I see the cruel cross,
I contemplate how much it cost
The holy One to suffer for me.
The Lamb of God, the innocent,
You bore my guilt and punishment:
My ransom's paid and I'm forgiven.

Now by Your blood You've overcome,
The victory over death is won;
So tell me, death, where is your sting?
A greater day is drawing near
When on the clouds You will appear,
To fetch Your bride and take her home.

So when I see the open tomb,
I realise I'm raised with You,
Forever now seated in heaven.
Before Your throne for endless days
We'll worship You and sing Your praise,
And cast our crowns down at Your feet.

2046

Tim Hughes & Ben Cantelon

THE GREATEST DAY IN HISTORY,
Death is beaten, You have rescued me.
Sing it out: Jesus is alive.
The empty cross, the empty grave,

Life eternal, You have won the day.
Shout it out: Jesus is alive,
He's alive.

And oh, happy day, happy day,
You washed my sin away.
Oh, happy day, happy day,
I'll never be the same.
Forever I am changed.

When I stand in that place,
Free at last, meeting face to face,
I am Yours, Jesus, You are mine.
Endless joy, perfect peace,
Earthly pain finally will cease.
Celebrate, Jesus is alive,
He's alive.

Oh, what a glorious day,
What a glorious way
That You have saved me.
And oh, what a glorious day,
What a glorious name,
Yeah, yeah, yeah, yeah.

2047

Reuben Morgan

THE HEAVENS DECLARE the glory of God,
And all of the world will join the praise,
His wonders proclaim.

The oceans and skies lift up their voice,
And all He has made will rise to bless
The King of all kings.

Let us adore Him,
Let us adore Him:
Jesus Christ is the Lord.
Come and behold Him,
Bow down before Him:
Jesus Christ is the Lord.

Eternity's King is coming again;
Though all of the earth will fade away,
His truth will remain.

Hallelujah, hallelujah,
You are worthy of all praise.
(Repeat)

2048

Johnny Parks & Phil Mawhinney

THE LORD IS CLOSE TO THE BROKEN-HEARTED,
The ones who feel crushed.
His ears attentive to our cries,
He will deliver us.

We'll draw near, seek Your face
In the sun, in the rain.
Upon our lips will be Your praise,
We'll rejoice in these days.

You've opened up my eyes.
I've seen You, Lord, and You are good.

We look to You, You uncover our face
And take away our shame.
We seek You, Lord, You answer us
And take away our fears.

2049

Graham Kendrick

THE LORD IS PRESENT HERE, *(x3)*
Come worship.
The Lord is present here, *(x3)*
Come worship.

Brought near by Jesus' blood, *(x3)*
We worship.
With angels round Your throne, *(x3)*
We worship.

We offer up our lives,
A living sacrifice,
Pouring out our gifts
Of thanks and praise.
This is Your holy hill,
You call us higher still,
Joining with all heaven
To proclaim:

Holy, holy, holy Lord,
God of power and might,
Heaven and earth are full
Of Your glory.

Let all the nations come *(x3)*
And worship.
Let all creation bow *(x3)*
In worship.

2050

Andrew Mitchell

THE LORD OUR GOD IS SEARCHING
Far across the land,
He's looking for the faithful,
A remnant who will stand.

His word of truth anointed,
That from their mouths impart
The mighty power of Jesus' name
To every human heart.

He's looking for the faithful,
The sons and heirs of grace,
To stand upon the mountains
And call to every race,
And to lead His people onward
Into His courts of praise,
Full of wonder, full of worship,
Full of faith.

Come on and sing, sing to the Lord!
A mighty awakening is all that we want.
We rise up in faith and cry out for more.
Send down a flood, revive us again,
Awaken us, Lord!

Could you be a disciple,
A bearer of the cross,
Steeped within the blood of Christ,
A lover of the lost?
So be ready for the journey
And run towards the goal,
Full of wonder, full of worship,
Full of hope.

2051

Noel & Tricia Richards & Wayne Drain

THERE ARE NO SECRET PLACES
Where I can hide.
You see my heart so clearly,
What goes on inside.
Nothing in this life
Can keep me from Your love.

For You are always, always loving me,
Love beyond all measure.
Always, always I will be
So in love with You,
So in love with You.

Your love goes on forever,
Never growing cold.
Your love is ever faithful,
Guards my heart and soul.
Nothing in this world
Can steal this love from me.

2052

Chris Tomlin, Matt Redman & Ed Cash

Inspired by the Robert Lowry hymn 'How can I keep from singing?' c. 1860

THERE IS AN ENDLESS SONG
Echoes in my soul;
I hear the music ring.
And though the storms may come
I am holding on;
To the rock I cling.

How can I keep from singing Your praise?
How can I ever say enough,
How amazing is Your love?
How can I keep from shouting Your name?
I know I am loved by the King,
And it makes my heart want to sing.

I will lift my eyes
In the darkest night,
For I know my Saviour lives.
And I will walk with You,
Knowing You see me through,
And sing the songs You give.

I can sing in the troubled times,
Sing when I win;
I can sing when I lose my step
And I fall down again.
I can sing 'cause You pick me up,
Sing 'cause You're there;
I can sing 'cause You hear me, Lord,
When I call to You in prayer.
I can sing with my last breath,
Sing for I know
That I'll sing with the angels
And the saints around the throne.

2053

Mark Tedder & Jeff Caylor

THERE IS A PLACE where water flows
And runs into the sea.
I want to go, I want to go
Where the river flows.

And there is a place where mercy flows
And runs into my heart.
I want to be, I want to be
Where Your mercy flows.

So lay me down in Your green pastures,
Let me rest beside Your streams.
When I walk, guide my footsteps
And I won't be afraid,
And I won't be afraid.

There is a place where glory falls
And covers the earth.
I want to be, I want to be
Where Your glory falls.

2054

Godfrey Birtill

THERE IS A PROMISE
Across this field,
A hope that's living,
A hope that's real.
There is a blessing
That breaks the curse:
It's life eternal, eternal,
Jesus Christ has won for us.

There is a rainbow
Over this land
That speaks a promise
To all mankind.
There is a mercy,
New every day:
Great is His faithfulness, His faithfulness,
Jesus Christ has saved the day.

2055

Matt Maher

THERE IS A TIME TO LIVE,
There is a time to die.
There is a time to laugh,
There is a time to cry.
There is a time to dance,
A time for joy's embrace,
And in all seasons, God,
We humbly seek Your face.

This is our offering to You,
This is our offering.

Everything I am is for Your glory,
Everything I am for You, Lord.
(Repeat)

There is a time to sow,
There is a time to reap.
A time for victory,
A time to claim defeat.
A time to be renewed,
A time to be reborn.
In all seasons, God,
We bow before Your throne.

The earth stands still without You.
We could only move because You made us to.
The world is nothing without You.
We could only love because You made us to.

2056

Stuart Barbour

THERE IS ONLY ONE GOD,
There is only one King.
There is only one God,
My Lord of everything.
Saviour to all the lost,
Redeemer for my soul.
A sovereign mighty God,
A Father to us all.

His name is Jesus,
Messiah,
My soul longs to sing.
His name is Jesus,
Messiah,
Master and King,
Master and King.

2057

Godfrey & Gill Birtill

THERE'S A BATTLE RAGING over this land,
A deep damage in the people.
Yet pride stops us
Stretching out our withered hand.
Yet God has stretched out to heal us.
This I know, this I know,
This I know, this I know:

That just one touch from the King
Changes everything.
Just one touch from the King
Changes everything.

There's a great darkness over this land,
A deep darkness on the people.
But a light is shining
That the dark can't understand:
Light of the world, King Jesus.
Do you know? Do you know?
Do you know? Do you know:

O land, O land, O land,
Hear the word of the Lord.
(Repeat)

2058

Geraldine Latty & busbee

THERE'S A DANCE that all creation
Is invited to join,
Where the Father, Son and Spirit
Interact and combine.
It's a dance where everyone can
Contribute to the whole
In the Spirit, through the Saviour,
To the Father.

With our minds and with our heart and strength,
Yes, all we can bring,
We are welcomed and included
In the dance of the King.
What astonishing salvation
That has come to our aid,
In the Spirit, through the Saviour,
To the Father.

La la la la la la la la,
La la la la la la la la.
(Repeat)
This is the dance full of glorious diversity.
This is the dance of our God.

In the Spirit, with the Saviour,
We will worship You, God,
Looking through Your eyes of mercy
To the world that You love.
And the dance that takes us into
Your compassion and grace
Will return us to the mission
Of the Father.

Join the worldwide celebration
With our God, three in one.
For this dance of liberation is
For all who will come.
And the wonder of this moment
Is that we now belong
In the Spirit, through the Saviour,
To the Father.

(Last time)
This is the dance full of glorious diversity.
This is the dance in the mystery of the Trinity.
This is the dance of our God.

2059

Raymond Badham

THERE'S A LIGHT IN THE DARKNESS that shines,
Giving hope to all the world,
Hope to all the world.
There's a door that's been opened to all,
Into a new and living way,
A new and living way.

Praise the name of Jesus,
Perfect Redeemer, star of the morning.
Yesterday, today and forever,
Jesus the same,
Jesus the same.

Your word is a lamp to my feet
And a light to my path,
A light to my path.
And so I run in the way of the truth:
There is freedom within,
Freedom within.

There's a fire that burns in our hearts,
To see the lost return to the Father.
It's a passion that's not of our own;
We have seen it in the Son,
In the face of the Son.

2060

Godfrey Birtill

THERE'S A LOT OF PAIN, but a lot more healing;
There's a lot of trouble, but a lot more peace.
There's a lot of hate, but a lot more loving;
There's a lot of sin, but a lot more grace.

Oh, outrageous grace!
Oh, outrageous grace!
Love unfurled by heaven's hand.
Oh, outrageous grace!
Oh, outrageous grace!
Through my Jesus I can stand.

There's a lot of fear, but a lot more freedom;
There's a lot of darkness, but a lot more light.
There's a lot of cloud, but a lot more vision;
There's a lot of perishing, but a lot more life.

There's an enemy
That seeks to kill what it can't control.
It twists and turns,
Making mountains out of mole hills.
But I will call on the Lord,
Who is worthy of praise;
I run to Him and I am saved.

2061

Robert Critchley

THERE'S A TIME to laugh
And a time to cry;
There's a time to mourn
And a time to shout for joy.
There's a time to gather in
And a time to give away;
For a season we may sow in tears,
Longing for the harvest day.

But it's always the time to worship You,
And it's always the time
To give our thanks to You.
We will praise Your name,
Jesus, faithful and true,
'Cause it's always the time to worship You,
Always the time.

There's a time for peace
And a time for war;
There's a time to rend
And a time to mend what's torn.
There's a time to fight for good
And a time for love's embrace;
For a season we may sacrifice
For the sake of brighter days.

There are many things in these troubled times
That can fill us with distress,
But when our eyes are on You, Jesus,
Then our hearts remain at rest.

2062

Simon Brading

THERE'S NO CONDEMNATION;
In this salvation I'm free.
Sin I was slave to,
Now has no power over me.

I don't deserve it, have not earned it;
It's Your grace on me,
And now my heart is free.

I'm alive in Jesus Christ,
And I know it's not 'cause of me.
Jesus, Your light has opened my eyes,
I'm free.

Objects of wrath,
Redeemed at the cross from our sin.
Chosen and living,
Forever forgiven by Him.

Jesus, Your blood
Will speak of Your love for all time.
Grace for today
And hope for tomorrow is mine.

It's a celebration of Your grace,
Celebration of Your grace;
With a song of love and a shout of praise,
Celebration.
(Repeat)

2063

Zimbabwean (Author unknown)
English translation: Hazel Chawafambira & Peter Gunstone

THERE'S NO ONE, THERE'S NO ONE LIKE JESUS;
There's no one, there's no one like Him.
There's no one, there's no one like Jesus;
There's no one, there's no one like Him.

We've run, we've run all over, all over.
We've looked, we've looked all over, all over.
We've travelled, travelled all over, all over;
There's no one, there's no one like Him.

Hakuna wakaita sa Jesu, hakuna wakaita saye.
Hakuna wakaita sa Jesu, haku, hakuchina.
Ndase, kwese.
Ndatsva*ga, tsvaga kwese, kwese.
Nda tenderera kwese, kwese.
Haku, hakuchina.

* 'tsva' may be pronounced like 'tch'

2064

Tim Hughes

THE RISING SUN that fills the sky,
The starry host that lights the night,
Reflecting Your glory.
The mountain heights forever stand,
The rain that falls to soak the land
Respond to Your glory.

Almighty God, in every way
You are above and beyond understanding.
If we did not praise, the rocks would cry out;
Glorious God, high above understanding.

The vast expanse of earth and sea,
Held by You in harmony,
Speaks of Your glory.
All You've made since time began,
Life itself Your perfect plan;
And it's all for Your glory.

Creation joins as one to sing,
'Glorious God',
So far above all earthly things.

2065

Chris Tomlin, Jesse Reeves & Ed Cash

THE SPLENDOUR OF THE KING,
Clothed in majesty;
Let all the earth rejoice,
All the earth rejoice.
He wraps Himself in light,
And darkness tries to hide,
And trembles at His voice,
And trembles at His voice.

How great is our God, sing with me,
How great is our God, and all will see
How great, how great is our God.

And age to age He stands,
And time is in His hands;
Beginning and the end,
Beginning and the end.
The Godhead, three in one,
Father, Spirit, Son,
The Lion and the Lamb,
The Lion and the Lamb.

Name above all names,
Worthy of all praise;
My heart will sing:
How great is our God.
(Repeat)

2066

Simon Brading

THE STARS IN THEIR COURSES ABOVE
Shine for Your glory: You alone are God.
By You every mountain was formed
To tell of Your story: You alone are God.
Eternally worthy of praise,
We join with creation and sing:

Lord, for all that You are,
For all that You've done,
I will praise You.
Lord, for all that You are,
For all that You'll do,
I will praise You.

The roar of Your thunder and rain
Tell of Your power: You alone are God.
The people You've called and redeemed

Bow in surrender: You alone are God.
Eternally worthy of praise,
We join with creation and sing:

Never ending, unfailing,
Everlasting, unfading,
(Repeat)
You are.

2067 Reuben Morgan

THE WHOLE EARTH overflowing
With Your power and Your glory;
There is no one like You, God.
There is no one like You, God.

Mountains bow, nations tremble;
At Your feet we cry 'Holy'.
There is no one like You, God.
There is no one like You, God.

Let creation sing
Of the risen King,
Let the universe resound.
With a shout of love
We will give to You
All the highest praise.

Let Your light shine upon us,
Let Your light shine upon us,
For the glory of Your name
Will be over all the earth.

Forever,
Forever I'll sing.
(Repeat)

2068

Stuart Garrard, Tim Jupp, Matt Redman, Martin Smith, Stewart Smith & Jonathan Thatcher

THE WINDS ARE BLOWING through again,
So we must follow –
A people daring to believe
We can change tomorrow,
And be the miracle of light,
And we won't give up the fight.

Now is the time for us to shine,
Shine with the face of Christ divine.
No compromise, for all heaven cries,
'Now is the time.'

The river's running through again,
Rejuvenating.
For everything You touch You change,
And we've all been changing.
We're a city shining on a hill,
Tell this world You're shining still.
Tell this world You're shining still.

Jesus, Jesus,
Precious Jesus, King of lights.
Jesus, Jesus,
Raise a church that's shining bright.

I want to follow, but what does it mean
To live in this world
And keep everything clean?
Nothing I own here is ever my own,
When I live in Your mercy and blessing You've shown.
I lay down my rights,
See the world through Your eyes,
And fight for the hungry,
Who pay for our lives.

I want to have You in all of my world,
So, Jesus, consume me, flow through me,
'Cause now is the time.

2069

Robin Mark

THE WONDER OF YOUR CROSS
Shall be our meditation,
To gather in that shadow
As the sun went down;
To weep with those who thought
That You were leaving,
You were leaving, Jesus,
The humble King
Who never wore an earthly crown.

To steal away at night
When they took down Your body,
With love and tears
To leave You in a borrowed grave;
To go with Mary to that place they laid You,
Where they laid You, Jesus,
And in the morning
Find the stone was rolled away.

The cross, oh, the wonderful cross;
What glory, what victory I've found.
I'll come to the wonderful cross
And my whole life I lay down.

Were heaven's praises silent
In those hours of darkness?
Your Holy Spirit
Brooding round that empty throne?
Until the declaration 'He is risen',
You are risen, Jesus:
'He is not dead,
Behold He lives forever more.'

2070

Andrew Mitchell

THE WORLD WILL CHANGE, its glories fade;
Our riches gone, but You remain.

The desert winds may dry the plains,
But aching hearts know You will reign.

Good Shepherd, come and find the lost.
Make haste the day You come again.

Your majesty, Lord,
Fills the whole earth,
Your royal train falls
And covers us all.
We will love You,
King forever;
We worship Jesus
And long for days
When You will return.

And as for me, I bring my all,
And count as gain all I thought loss.
So take my life and let me be
Evermore near to Thee.

2071

Máire Brennan & Keith Getty

THIS FRAGILE VESSEL You have made,
No hand on earth can fill,
For the waters of this world have failed
And I am thirsty still.

We can be worthy of His love,
Wisdom and mercy.

Take this bread and wine;
As we share His cross and crown,
Receive the grace sent down.

I seek the treasures of Your love,
It's not that far to see.
I heard a melody above,
A gift from You to me.

To save what's lost from heaven He came,
His presence still remains;
Open our eyes to His precious blood,
Because it's not in vain.

2072

Matt Redman

THIS IS A GIFTED RESPONSE;
Father, we cannot come to You
By our own merit.
We will come in the name of Your Son,
As He glorifies You,
And in the power of Your Spirit.

We have come to something so mysterious,
Too deep for minds to comprehend;
Through the open door where the angels sing
And the host of heaven are antheming.

And we'll sing the glory of Your name,
Celebrate the glories of Your grace.
We will worship You, we will worship You.
And we'll make Your praise so glorious,
Singing songs of everlasting praise.
We will worship You, we will worship You.

2073

David Gate

THIS IS HOW I KNOW WHAT LOVE IS,
This is how I know what love is;
Jesus took the cross in mercy –
A love I don't deserve.

Extravagant, magnificent,
The love You pour on me.
Extravagant, magnificent,
Your grace I have received.

Now everything I am must praise You,
Everything I am must praise You.
Everything I have I give You –
A life You so deserve.

This is how I know what love is,
This is how I know what love is;
It's only by the grace of Jesus,
It's only by the grace of Jesus.

2074

Johnny Parks & Phil Mawhinney

THIS IS MY, MY RESPONSE:
A humble prayer lifted up;
A prayer of thanks for who You are.
You're the One, the One who lights the world,
You're the One who lights the world,
You're the One who lights the world.

Show Yourself to me, Lord.
Come and illuminate.
Your light uncovers the face of God.
Light up, O Lord.
Light up, O Lord.
Light up, O Lord.

This is my, my response:
Thankful hands lifted up;
A heartfelt act that points to You.
Let, let my light be true,
Let my light be true,
Let my light be true.

2075

Noel & Tricia Richards

THIS IS OUR GREATEST JOY:
To know that we are Yours.
We live to worship You,
The Lord most high.
Maker of this world,
You formed us from the dust.
Our lives will honour You,
Our voices sing:

Hallelujah, hallelujah,
We cry hallelujah.

You left Your Father's home,
Into our world You came;
The innocent who bore
Our guilt and shame.
When You gave Your life
The victory was won.
With thankful hearts we sing
This song of praise:

Your light of life has come,
Your Spirit makes us strong.
Great hope for all the world
Through all You've done.
We will worship You,
We will applaud Your ways;
Into Your presence come
With songs of praise:

2076

Matt Redman

THIS IS THE ANTHEM OF THE FREE,
This is the song of the redeemed,
Jesus, Your praises rising
Higher and higher and higher.
We'll sing it loud, we'll sing it strong,
We'll sing it all around the world.
Jesus, Your praise will last
Forever and ever and ever.

Hear the sound of the free,
Hear the cry of liberty.
We will rejoice in You,
We will rejoice.
As we sing of all You've done
And the wonders of Your love,
We will rejoice in You,
We will rejoice.

Rising up around the earth
Is a heavenly song of Your endless worth,
Growing louder and louder and louder.

Then one day Your heavenly song
Will drown all music but its own.
Then one day Your heavenly song
Will drown all music but its own.
(Repeat)

2077

Andrew Mitchell

THIS IS THE DAY the Lord has made;
We will rejoice and be glad.
Even the trees of the fields clap their hands,
As all God's people sing with joy.

This is the day the Lord has made;
We will rejoice and be glad in it.
If darkness overcomes me
I know You'll light the way.
This is the day the Lord has made.

And on this day that You have made,
Fill our hearts with holy fire,
That we may live by the power of Your name
And show the world that You're alive.

Let us go up to the house of the Lord.
Let us go up singing praises to God!
(Repeat)

2078

Andrew Mitchell

THIS IS THE SWEETEST PLACE
I could surely know,
And here I'll spend my days
Worshipping the Lord.

And in this sweetest place,
Whatever I've been through,
Arms that never fail
Reach for me anew.

You are the morning star that heralds dawn,
You're the rock of love I'm founded on
And the shelter that I run to, Lord.
It's the sweetest place,
The very sweetest place of all.

2079

Simon Brading

THOUGH I WALK upon ground
That is rugged and uneven,
Your faithful hand
Won't lead me astray.
Through the rain and the clouds,
Where the sun is barely shining,
Your grace surrounds my life every day,
Every day.

You reign yesterday, today,
Forever more, forever more.
You reign in every circumstance.
You are good, You are good.

And You hold in Your hands
Every star, the sun and moon,
Yet those hands are marred
And wounded from nails.
Precious blood at the cross
Was poured out for the nations,
And this love that drove salvation never fails.
Your love never fails.

You rule the world,
You rule the world, You reign.
You are the Name above all names,
The King above all kings, You reign.

2080

Martyn Layzell

THOUGH THE BLOSSOM does not bloom
And though the fields produce no food,
A song I will sing to Jesus my King.
When the wine has all run dry

And there's no fruit upon the vine,
In You I rejoice, I lift up my voice.
When my faith in You
Is fading out of view:

I'm holding on, I'm holding on,
I'm holding on to You.

In sorrow and in suffering,
In trials and through tragedy,
To Jesus I cling – You're my everything.
In weakness and adversity,
Sufficient is Your grace for me;
In You I will trust as You lift me up.
When my faith in You
Is fading out of view:

For when I'm weak, then I am strong;
You're all I need to carry on.
I will not fear, for You are here,
O Lord, O Lord.

2081

Rex Allchurch

THROUGH EVERYTHING I DO,
No matter where I may go,
I want to be close to You,
I want to be serving You.

'Cause it is my heart's
And it is my soul's one desire
To worship You.
Yeah, it is my heart's
And it is my soul's one desire
To worship You.

Can I carry the fragrance of God,
And people see me through Your love?
That I could know Your fullness, God,
Give everything back to You.

2082

Martyn Layzell

THROUGH YOUR PRECIOUS BLOOD
You have bought peace,
Dying on a cross,
Born to set man free.
Emptying Yourself
Of all majesty,
Came into this world,
A light for all to see.
What love! What sacrifice!
With You I'm reconciled.

Not to us,
But unto You be the glory.
Forever You will be,
Forever You will be exalted.
Your great love,
The only way to the Father.
Your Spirit lives in me,
And now I live to tell Your story.

Now we have this hope
Filling our souls;
Love so undeserved,
Grace now overflows.
So with confidence
We boldly approach;
Through the blood You shed
We've access to Your throne.
What love! What sacrifice!
With You I'm reconciled.

Jesus, You are worthy,
Jesus, You are worthy.
Only You deserve all the glory.
(Repeat)

2083

Brian Doerksen & Sandra Gage

TODAY I CHOOSE to follow You.
Today I choose to give my 'yes' to You.
Today I choose to hear Your voice and live.
Today I choose to follow You.

As for me and my house,
We will serve You.
As for me and my house,
We will spend our lives on You
Today.

Wonderful Counsellor,
Everlasting Father.
Eternal King, Lord of hosts,
Willingly we follow.

2084

Raymond Badham

TOGETHER IN THIS PLACE of worship
Your greatness we proclaim;
We stand as one in giving You
All glory and acclaim.
To You our hearts are open,
To You our hands we raise.
Come take the place of honour
In our lives.

Emmanuel,
Our God is with us.
Prince of Peace, mighty One,
The ever-living God.
(Repeat)

See the praises of our Saviour
Rise to open skies.
With the dawning of redemption,
Your glory will arise.
For You alone are worthy,
Here in Zion You are praised.
Our Lord and King,
Forever You will reign.

2085 Brian Doerksen, Michael Hansen & Brian Thiessen

TO THE RIVER I am going,
Bringing sins I cannot bear.
Come and cleanse me, come forgive me;
Lord, I need to meet You there.

In these waters healing mercy
Flows with freedom from despair.
I am going to that river;
Lord, I need to meet You there.

Precious Jesus, I am ready
To surrender every care.
Take my hand now, lead me closer;
Lord, I need to meet You there.

Come and join us in the river,
Come, find life beyond compare.
He is calling, He is waiting;
Jesus longs to meet you there.

2086

Nick Herbert & Matt Redman

TRIBES PRAISING, tongues singing
Now before Your throne.
Your anthem will drown
All music but its own.

Hosts on high glorify
Your most holy name,
With elders and creatures
Gathered to proclaim.

Crown Him with many crowns,
Crown Him with many crowns,
Crown Him with many crowns,
The Lamb upon the throne.

Eyes gazing, hearts waiting,
As our King draws near.
Souls stirring, as You reveal
Your presence here.

Lift up your hearts,
Lift up your lives;
It's right to give Him thanks and praises.
(Repeat)

2087

Brenton Brown & Brian Doerksen

TRIUNE GOD, uncreated,
Perfect three in one.
Sacred bond, humble friendship,
Living dance of light.
Draw our lives into the wonder of . . .

Your majesty,
Your fellowship divine;
The Spirit's liberty,
The grace of Jesus Christ.
The Father's faithful love,
The sharing of Your life
In holy communion,
One God.

2088

Martyn Layzell

TURN MY FACE AGAIN towards the cross
On the mount of Calvary.
Take me back again to ponder on
The life You gave,
The price You paid to save me.

Kneel me down again before the cross
Where they pierced Your hands and feet.
King so humble in a crown of thorns,
The scars You wear
Were mine to bear forever.

O Jesus, I could never be the same;
I'm changed forever more.
Your sacrifice, the key to life for all mankind,
You did it once for all.

Lead me to the place Your body lay,
Where the stone lies rolled away.
Clothed in majesty and victory,
You rose again
And death is slain forever.

You did it once for all. *(x2)*

2089

David Crowder

TURN YOUR EAR TO HEAVEN
And hear the noise inside;
The sound of angels' awe,
The sound of angels' songs.
And all this for a King;
We could join and sing,
All to Christ the King.

How constant, how divine,
This song of ours will rise.
Oh, how constant, how divine,
This love of ours will rise, will rise.

O praise Him, O praise Him:
He is holy, He is holy, yeah.

Turn your gaze to heaven
And raise a joyous noise;
The sound of salvation come,
The sound of rescued ones.
And all this for a King,
Angels join to sing,
All for Christ the King.

How infinite and sweet,
This love so rescuing.
Oh, how infinitely sweet,
This great love that has redeemed.
As one we sing.

Alleluia, alleluia:
He is holy, He is holy, yeah.

2090

Helen Lemmel
Adpt. by Vicky Beeching & Christopher Stevens

TURN YOUR EYES UPON JESUS,
Look full in His wonderful face;
And the things of earth
Will grow strangely dim
In the light of His glory and grace,
In the light of His glory and grace.

Isn't He beautiful?
Isn't He beautiful?
Outshining sun and stars,
It's indescribable
How breathtaking You are.

So I turn my eyes upon You now,
Look full in Your wonderful face;
And the things of earth,
They grow strangely dim
In the light of Your glory and grace,
In the light of Your glory and grace.

You are so beautiful.
You are so beautiful.
Outshining sun and stars,
It's indescribable
How breathtaking You are.

2091

David Gate

UNAPPROACHABLE LIGHT,
So bright it is frightening,
Holiness shining.
You're the purest of lights,

Can't see without dying,
There is no hiding.
Just glimpses we see today,
But in heaven we'll see Your face:

Where no heart will deny
The beauty of Christ
Seated on high.
And all tongues will proclaim
Your worth and Your fame,
For eternity to reign,
There will only be one name.

2092

Godfrey Birtill

UNBELIEF IS A BARREN FIELD
In a strange land:
Nothing lives there.
Unbelief is a deep hole
Full of heavy clay:
I don't want to be there.
I will rise up from my unbelief,
Up to the place of faith;
To fly up high on eagles' wings
By grace.

I will fan the flame of faith,
Fan the flame of faith,
Fan the flame of faith again.
(Repeat)

Lost hope is a weary mind,
It's a sickened heart,
A stolen vision.
Lost hope is a downcast soul,
It's the bitter taste
Of disappointment.

But I know a hope that's coming,
Hope that is a tree of life.
So I'm trusting in the living hope,
Jesus Christ.

2093

Nick Herbert & Tim Hughes

WAKE EVERY HEART and every tongue
To sing the new eternal song,
And crown Him King of glory now,
Confess Him Lord of all.

You are the highest, You are the greatest,
You are the Lord of all.
Angels will worship, nations will bow down
To the Lord of all.

The day will come when all will sing
And glorify our matchless King.
Your name unrivalled stands alone:
You are the Lord of all.

Let every heart, let every tongue
Sing of Your name, sing of Your name.
Let every heart, let every tongue
Sing, sing, sing.
(Repeat)

We're lifting You higher,
Higher and higher,
Lifting You higher,
Higher and higher,
Lifting You higher,
Higher and higher, O Lord.
(Repeat)

2094

Andrew Mitchell

WALK WITH ME, LORD, through the dawn,
Show me Your mercies new;
The deep in You calls and I long to be
A vessel of honour for You.

Walk with me, Lord, through the noon,
When it feels like my strength has all gone.
Help me to focus my eyes on You,
And comfort me, Lord, when I fall.

Amazed by Your love, I'm broken inside.
I cannot deny You, O Lord of my life.
I give You my heart and freely I choose
To follow You, Jesus, all of my life through.

Walk with me late in the day,
When my spirit is weary with toil;
I will sing a new song of my faithful God,
And the morning will bring me joy.

2095

Eoghan Heaslip & Matt Redman

WANDERERS IN THIS WILDERNESS,
Yet we find our home in You.
Strangers in a foreign land,
Yet we find our hope in You.

When all else changes, You remain.
You've always been our dwelling place,
O Lord.

We find grace in the wilderness,
Strength enough to sing
Of Your unfailing love.

You are close, closer than we know,
And there will be a day
When all will be revealed.

Before the mountain peaks were formed,
Before the earth itself was born;
From the beginning to the end
You have always been our God.

2096

Gareth Robinson

WE ADORE YOU, LORD,
We sing You our praise,
For You are wonderful, beautiful,
How lovely is Your name.

We exalt You, Lord,
We glorify Your name,
For You are powerful, merciful,
How lovely is Your name.

Hallelujah, hallelujah,
Hallelujah, Lord.
(Repeat)

Jesus, we love Your name. *(x4)*

2097

Lynn DeShazo & Gary Sadler

WE ARE A MOMENT, You are forever,
Lord of the ages, God before time.
We are a vapour, You are eternal,
Love everlasting, reigning on high.

Holy, holy, Lord God Almighty,
Worthy is the Lamb that was slain.
Highest praises, honour and glory
Be unto Your name,
Be unto Your name.

We are the broken, You are the healer,
Jesus Redeemer, mighty to save.
You are the love song we'll sing forever,
Bowing before You, blessing Your name.

2098

Ian Hannah

WE ARE BOWED BEFORE YOU,
Our hearts are open wide;
Lord, would You visit us again?
We are desperate people,
Who long to feel Your hand;
Would You come in power and break in?

Fill this house,
Fill this place,
Fill this temple of praise;
Show us Your glory.
Fill this house,
Fill this place,
Fill this temple of praise;
Show us Your glory.
Show us Your glory.

May our eyes be opened
To Your everlasting hope;
May Your Spirit captivate our lives.
Deeper revelation,
A closer walk with You;
Filled with passion we will rise.

2099

John L. Bell & Graham Maule

WE CANNOT MEASURE HOW YOU HEAL
Or answer every sufferer's prayer,
Yet we believe Your grace responds
Where faith and doubt unite to care.
Your hands, though bloodied on the cross,
Survive to hold and heal and warn,
To carry all through death to life
And cradle children yet unborn.

The pain that will not go away,
The guilt that clings from things long past,
The fear of what the future holds
Are present as if meant to last.
But present too is love which tends
The hurt we never hoped to find,
The private agonies inside,
The memories that haunt the mind.

So some have come who need Your help,
And some have come to make amends:
Your hands which shaped and saved the world
Are present in the touch of friends.
Lord, let Your Spirit meet us here
To mend the body, mind and soul,
To disentangle peace from pain
And make Your broken people whole.

2100

Timothy Dudley-Smith

WE COME AS GUESTS INVITED
When Jesus bids us dine,
His friends on earth united
To share the bread and wine;

The bread of life is broken,
The wine is freely poured
For us in solemn token
Of Christ our dying Lord.

We eat and drink, receiving
From Christ the grace we need,
And in our hearts believing
On Him by faith we feed;
With wonder and thanksgiving
For love that knows no end,
We find in Jesus living
Our ever-present friend.

One bread is ours for sharing,
One single fruitful vine,
Our fellowship declaring
Renewed in bread and wine;
Renewed, sustained and given
By token, sign and word,
The pledge and seal of heaven,
The love of Christ our Lord.

2101

Gareth Robinson

WE COME TO BE WITH YOU TODAY, our God.
We come to bring the praise that You deserve.
Thanksgiving, hands clapping,
Mouths singing, living
To worship You with heart and soul
And mind and strength.

Praise You, Lord,
For all that You are.
Praise You, Lord,
For all that You've done.
Praise You, Lord,
For all that You've made us to be.

We come together as Your people now.
We come united by the Saviour's blood.
Peace-making, hands serving,
Mouths blessing, living
By grace to love our neighbour
As we love ourselves.

By grace we have been saved through faith,
And faith is Your gift which we now receive.
(Repeat)

2102

Mark Tedder, John Hartley, Chris Donohue & Tom Lane

WE DON'T KNOW WHAT TOMORROW HOLDS,
But we know who holds tomorrow.
We can't see what's down the road,
But we know who holds our hand.

Your mercy will attend us,
Your glory will surround us,
The mighty hand of God is on our side.

Without Your presence, O Lord,
We will not go from here;
We're standing in the place of perfect rest.
Show us Your glory and teach us Your ways,
So we will know the favour of the Lord.

We are set apart for the pleasure of the Lord,
To proclaim that Jesus is the King.
We can't see what's down the road,
But we know who holds our hand.

2103

Paul Oakley

WE GIVE THANKS to You, Almighty God,
The One who was and is to come.
You've taken up Your power
And You've begun to reign.
All the nations bow before You,
And the saints revere Your name.

The kingdoms of this world belong to You,
And all authority is Yours.
You have purchased men
From every tribe and tongue,
And You're making us a people
Who will glorify the Son.

Because You have become our salvation:
You alone are worthy, Jesus.
Yours is the power
And the kingdom:
You alone are God,
And You reign forever.

A battle rages in the heavenlies,
And the accuser is thrown down.
And loving not our lives even unto death,
By Your blood we overcome,
By Your blood we overcome.

2104

Martyn Layzell

WE HAVE HEARD THE CALL TO GO
Into the world with seed to sow.
With living words within our hearts,
We will walk as Jesus walked.

Live a life of sacrifice
And die to our human desires.
To see the poor and not pass by
Is to walk as Jesus walked.
Help us walk as Jesus walked.

But if not now, then when will we
Take up our cross and follow?
And if not us, then who will go
And walk as Jesus walked?

(Last chorus)
We will walk as You have walked.

Be good news in all we do,
Bind up the broken-hearted.
Heal the sick and raise the dead
Is to walk as Jesus walked.
Help us walk as Jesus walked.

With passion for the lost,
Compassion for the poor,
To every corner of the world,
We'll walk as You have walked.
A Father to the fatherless,
You're Father to them all.

2105

Matt Redman

WE HAVE NOTHING TO GIVE
That didn't first come from Your hand;
We have nothing to offer You
Which You did not provide.
Every good, perfect gift comes from
Your kind and gracious heart,
And all we do is give back to You
What always has been Yours.

Lord, we're breathing the breath
That You gave us to breathe,
To worship You, to worship You.
And we're singing these songs
With the very same breath,
To worship You, to worship You.

Who has given to You
That it should be paid back to him?
Who has given to You
As if You needed anything?
From You and to You and through You
Come all things, O Lord,
And all we do is give back to You
What always has been Yours.

We are breathing the breath
That You gave us to breathe.
(Repeat)

2106

Nathan & Lou Fellingham & busbee

WE HAVE THIS TREASURE from the Lord our God,
A gift of mercy from His hand;
His all-surpassing power at work in us,
To show His glory and His plan.
For He has offered hope to all mankind
Through sending Jesus to the cross;
And now this light He's shone into our hearts
We're holding out to all the world.

Now with His power in us we'll reign in life,
With eyes of faith we'll move ahead;
The Spirit helps and strengthens us each day,
Confirming our eternal place.
Our confidence is not our ability,

Nor in the earthly strength that we hold,
But in His grace He takes the fragile things,
To show the greatness of His love.

We will sing out, we will proclaim
The wonder and joy of His endless grace;
Drawing us on till Jesus comes again
To take His people home.

No longer living for this passing life,
We'll fix our eyes on what is sure:
There is a heavenly place prepared for us
That will not ever fade or spoil.
So we will walk the path He has given us,
In full obedience and with faith,
For when the road is tough we will not lose heart,
But keep on trusting in His name.

2107

Matt Redman

WELCOMED IN TO THE COURTS OF THE KING,
I've been ushered in to Your presence.
Lord, I stand on Your merciful ground,
Yet with every step tread with reverence.

There is none in the heavens like You,
And upon the earth, who's Your equal?
You are far above, You're the highest of heights,
I am bowing down to exalt You.

And I'll fall facedown
As Your glory shines around.
Yes, I'll fall facedown
As Your glory shines around.

Let Your glory shine around,
Let Your glory shine around,
King of glory, here be found,
King of glory.
(Repeat)
King of glory, King of glory.
King of glory, King of glory.

2108

Howard Francis

WELCOME IN THIS PLACE,
Welcome in this place.

We give to You the highest praise:
Welcome in this place.

2109

Steve Fortunato

WE LIFT OUR EYES TO YOU,
Higher than our own horizon.
We lift our voice to You,
Giving thanks for each provision.
This is our prayer,
This is our prayer,
This is our prayer:
Be magnified,
Be magnified.

You are our God,
We give You praise.
We take delight
In the sound of Your name.
Be magnified,
Be magnified.

Stories that we hold,
You already know the pages.
As our view unfolds,
We join in the song of ages.
This is our prayer,
This is our prayer,
This is our prayer:
Be magnified,
Be magnified.

2110

Chris Tomlin & Jesse Reeves

WE LIFT OUR HANDS in praise to You,
Lift our hearts in worship to You, Lord.
We lift our voice to You and sing:
Our greatest love will ever be You, Lord,
You, Lord.

Glorious, over us.
You shall reign glorious.

There is a King that we adore;
With humble hearts we bow before You, Lord.
There is a place we long to be;
Yes, face to face we long to see You, Lord,
You, Lord.

Majesty and power
Are Yours alone forever.
(Repeat)

2111

Lex Buckley & Tim Hughes

WE LOOK TO YOUR WORD
And see Your awesome faithfulness.
We look to the earth
And glimpse Your beauty.
We look to the stars
And see Your majesty displayed.
The heavens above declare Your glory.

We join with the angels,
Singing, 'Holy, holy, holy.'
We stand with creation,
Crying, 'Worthy is the Lord.'
Every knee shall bow,
And every tongue confess
That You are God.

We look to Your Son
And find a love that never fails.
We look to the cross
And see Your mercy.
We look to the grave,
Empty because You rose again.
Glorious One, You reign in power.

Holy, holy, holy is the Lord.
You reign in glory, glory,
You reign in glory forever more.

2112

Evan Rogers

WE REJOICE because You came from heaven to earth,
Laying down Your majesty in humble birth.
We rejoice because You have so loved the world;
You are Christ, Emmanuel.

We rejoice because You lived a perfect life;
With our frailty You have identified.
We rejoice because You came to make us whole.
You're the Shepherd of our souls.

Siyavuya kuwe.
Siyavuya kuwe.
Siyavuya kuwe.
Jesu Akekho fan' nawe.

(We rejoice in You.
We rejoice in You.
We rejoice in You.
Jesus, there is none like You.)

We are humbled that Your life led to the cross;
There You gave Yourself, a sacrifice for us.
We are humbled at the way You suffered pain,
Lamb of God for sinners slain.

I rejoice because You have forgiven my sin;
You received the Father's wrath – my punishment.
I rejoice because of Your amazing grace;
Now I'm free from guilt and shame.

We rejoice because You broke the curse of death;
Now we live in hope, sure of eternal rest.
We rejoice because You've made our home in heaven,
Where we'll worship You forever.

We rejoice because You sit at God's right hand,
And before Your throne we're lifting up Your name.
We'll rejoice when every tribe and tongue proclaims:
'Jesus is the Lord who reigns!'

2113

Mark Tedder

WE SING YOUR SONG when our passion is fading,
We sing Your song in a thirsty land.
We sing Your song when darkness surrounds,
We sing Your song over and over.

And we are the people of God,
Humbled and in awe.
Through the fire and the rain,
You, my God, will never change.
Kingdoms will fall,
But through it all,
We are the people of God.

We sing Your song when the world is changing,
We sing Your song when we don't understand.
We sing Your song when the battle is raging,
We sing Your song over and over.

We sing Your song in the stillness of night,
We sing Your song when our future's uncertain.
We sing Your song with a cry and a whisper,
We sing Your song over and over.

2114

Chris Tomlin & Louie Giglio

WE STAND AND LIFT UP OUR HANDS,
For the joy of the Lord is our strength.
We bow down and worship Him now;
How great, how awesome is He.

And together we sing,
Everyone sing:

Holy is the Lord God Almighty;
The earth is filled with His glory.
Holy is the Lord God Almighty;
The earth is filled with His glory,
The earth is filled with His glory.

It's rising up all around,
It's the anthem of the Lord's renown.
(Repeat)

2115

Dave Bilbrough

WE'VE COME TO SING our songs of worship.
We've come to give ourselves in praise;
To offer thanks to our Creator,
And celebrate the One who saves.

Everybody sing of His everlasting love.
Everybody sing of His everlasting love.
He's slow to anger, rich in mercy;
Let all the earth declare His glory.
Everybody sing of His everlasting love.

Alleluia! Alleluia!
(Repeat)
Everlasting love.

2116

Nigel Briggs

WE WAIT IN HOPE FOR YOU,
Our shelter and our truth.
You are always faithful to Your word.
Consume our hearts and minds,
Be the author of this life.
Your kingdom come, Your will be done.

In these times of doubt and sorrow
People need a hope to cling to.
Your love is an anchor in the storms of life,
Forever faithful.

Unfailing love,
You never let us down.
Your promise is alive.

When coloured dreams fade to grey:
Unfailing love.
When the night crowds out the day:
Unfailing love.
When there's no words left to say,
God's love remains.

2117

Nick Herbert

WE WORSHIP YOU,
Father in heaven.
Father in heaven,
You are holy.
Your will be done
As it is in heaven,
As it is in heaven,
As we forgive.

Give us all we need
This side of heaven.
Give us all we need today.

Yours is the kingdom,
Yours is the power,
Yours is the glory
Forever and ever, amen.

And grant that we
Might be forgiven,
Might be forgiven
As we forgive.
And lead us not
Into temptation,
And from temptation
Deliver us.

2118

Chris Tomlin, Sean Craig & Jesse Reeves

WHAT CAN TAKE A DYING MAN
And raise him up to life again?
What can heal a wounded soul?
What can make us white as snow?
What can fill the emptiness?
What can mend our brokenness,
Brokenness?

Mighty, awesome, wonderful
Is the holy cross,
Where the Lamb laid down His life
To lift us from the fall.
Mighty is the power of the cross.

What restores our faith in God?
What reveals the Father's love?
What can lead the wayward home?
What can melt a heart of stone?
What can free the guilty ones?
What can save and overcome,
Overcome?

It's a miracle to me,
It's a miracle to me,

And it's still a mystery,
And it's still a mystery.
It's a miracle to me,
The power of God
For those who believe.

2119

Tim & Rachel Hughes

WHAT GOOD IS IT TO GAIN THE WHOLE WORLD
But lose your soul?
What good is it to make a sweet sound
But remain proud?

In view of God's mercy,
I offer my all.

And take my life – let it be,
Everything, all of me.
Here I am – use me for Your glory.
In everything I say and do,
Let my life honour You.
Here I am, living for Your glory.

The road I'm on, it leads nowhere
Without You.
And the life I lead, it finds meaning
In surrender.

Seeking first the kingdom,
Seeking first the kingdom of my Lord.
(Repeat)

2120

Ian & Stuart Townend

WHAT LOVE HAS CAPTURED ME,
What mercy filled my soul,
That calls the sinner clean

And makes the wounded whole.
Too high for words to tell,
For minds to comprehend.

'Cause I'm filled with the life of God,
Thrilled with the Father's love,
And as I worship, my heart is filled
With wonder, with wonder.
Grateful that I should be
Part of Your family,
And as I worship, my heart is filled
With wonder, with wonder.

When hope abandons me
I call to mind what's true;
My faith is not in me
But what my God can do.
His words have power to turn
The night to glorious day.

2121

Joseph Irons (1785–1852) Adpt. by David Hyde
Music: Ian Hannah

WHAT SACRED FOUNTAIN freely springs up
From the throne of God,
And all new covenant blessing brings?
It's Jesus' precious blood.

What a mighty sum paid all my debt
When I a bankrupt stood,
And has my life in credit set.
It's Jesus' precious blood.

O precious blood, it covers me,
It takes away the stain of sin.
Such power there is contained within
Jesus' precious blood.

What stream is that, which sweeps away
My sin just like a flood,
So not a hint of it can stay?
It's Jesus' precious blood.

What voice is that which speaks for me
In heaven's high court for good,
And justifies and sets me free?
It's Jesus' precious blood.

What theme, my soul, shall best employ
Your song before your God,
And make all heaven ring for joy?
It's Jesus' precious blood.

2122

Andy Bromley

WHAT SHALL I BRING before the Lord,
And bow my knee before my God?
Extravagant sacrifice.
Can I give You a thousand words,
Or please You with ten thousand songs?
Extravagant sacrifice.

You have shown us what is good
Through the message of Your Son.

Show justice, love mercy,
Walk humbly with your God.
(Repeat)

My life I bring before the Lord,
And bow my knee before my God:
Extravagant sacrifice.
My love, more than a thousand words,
My praise, more than ten thousand songs:
Extravagant sacrifice.

You have shown us what is good,
Through the message of Your Son.
His life, His death poured out for us;
His word, His ways our life-blood.

2123

Gareth Robinson

WHEN ALL AROUND I FEEL DESPAIR
And all my hope is gone,
I look to Your eternal word,
Find strength to carry on.
Undying words of boundless grace
So freely poured on me,
I trust in each and every one
And walk on gratefully.

I put my confidence in You,
You tell me I'm secure,
And You'll provide for all my needs,
Through all that I endure.
Your words of life restore my hope,
A breath of clean fresh air;
So stronger do I take each step
And cast off all despair.

How great a gift that You should give
Your Son that I'd go free.
So ever shall I praise Your name
For all eternity.
No sorrow, fear or evil foe
Can steal Your love away.
Each day I hold on to Your word,
Your life, Your word, Your grace.

2124

Tim Hughes

WHEN ALL AROUND IS FADING
And nothing seems to last;
When each day is filled with sorrow,
Still I know with all my heart:

He's got the whole world in His hands,
He's got the whole world in His hands.
I'll fear no evil, for You are with me,
Strong to deliver, mighty to save.
He's got the whole world in His hands.

When I walk through fire,
I will not be burned;
When the waves come crashing round me,
Still I know with all my heart:

2125

Sammy Horner & Stuart Trotter

WHEN EVERYTHING IS UPHILL,
When everything is pain,
I find amazing comfort
When I recall again

That the nails that pierced His hands,
And the thorns that pierced His brow,
And the spear that pierced His side,
And the nails that pierced His feet
Showed us there can be
Victory in defeat.
And the stone that rolled away,
And the empty grave they found,
Where His perfumed grave-clothes lay
Folded on the ground,
A mystery so sweet,
Victory in defeat.

And in the darkest valley,
And in the time of fear,
When everything seems blurred,
The one thing that seems clear:

2126

Brenton Brown

WHEN I AM SINKING DOWN,
When I am lost at sea,
No solace to be found,
No ground beneath my feet;
I turn to You as I go down,
I reach for You through roaring waves.
My only hope is in Your arms,
My only prayer is that You'd save me.

'Cause You make me soar like the angels,
And You let me walk on the water,
And You let me run with white horses,
Jesus, my strength when all is gone.

When I am all alone,
No land is in my sight,
All others lost from view,
And comes the darkening night;
I reach for You as I go down,
I look to You through wind and waves.
My only hope is in Your arms,
My only prayer is that You'd save me.

2127

Ben Cantelon

WHEN I CALL ON YOUR NAME, You answer;
When I fall, You are there by my side.
You delivered me out of darkness,
Now I stand in the hope of new life.

By grace I'm free,
You've rescued me;
All I am is Yours.

I've found a love greater than life itself.
I've found a hope stronger and nothing compares.
I once was lost, now I'm alive in You.

You're my God and my firm foundation;
It is You whom I'll trust at all times.
I give glory and praise, adoration
To my Saviour who's seated on high.

Love came down and rescued me,
I thank You, I thank You.
I once was blind but now I see,
I see You, I see You.

2128

Andy Bromley

WHEN I GAZE UPON THE WONDERS OF THIS WORLD that You have made,
It's beautiful.
When I look above and see
An open sky that's full of stars
That You have named,
So beautiful.
And all that I can say to You:

You are beautiful in majesty,
In majesty.
How glorious Your praise,
How wonderful Your ways.
How majestic is Your name.
(Repeat)
Your majesty.

When I see a life transforming
By the power of Your grace,
It's beautiful.
When I hear the adoration
Of Your people lost in wonder,
Love and praise,
So beautiful.
And all that I can say to You:

When I think of where I was
And how You brought me to this place,
It's beautiful.
I'm so grateful, Lord, for all begun in me
You're faithful to complete,
So beautiful.
And all that I can say to You:

2129

Godfrey Birtill

WHEN I LOOK AT THE BLOOD,
All I see is love, love, love.
When I stop at the cross,
I can see the love of God.

But I can't see competition,
I can't see hierarchy.
I can't see pride or prejudice
Or the abuse of authority.
I can't see lust for power,
I can't see manipulation.
I can't see rage or anger
Or selfish ambition.

But I can't see unforgiveness,
I can't see hate or envy.
I can't see stupid fighting
Or bitterness or jealousy.

I can't see empire building,
I can't see self-importance.
I can't see back stabbing
Or vanity or arrogance.

And I see surrender, sacrifice,
Salvation, humility,
Righteousness, faithfulness,
Grace, forgiveness.
Love, love, love. *(x7)*

(Last time)
When I stop at the cross,
I can see the love of God.

2130

Tré & Tori Sheppard & Kathryn Scott

WHEN I NEED SOMEONE to quiet my fears
Till the whispers inside me all disappear;
When I need someone to dry all my tears,
I wait for You,
Yes, I wait for You.

When I taste sorrow, when pain is my friend,
When I can't hide what's broken, I can't pretend;
When all that I hoped for has faded again,
I wait for You,
Yes, I wait for You.

Love, rescue me. (x4)

This longing, this aching,
Only Your love can rescue me.
I'm calling, here waiting,
Oh, send Your love to rescue me.

2131

Paul Baloche & Graham Kendrick

WHEN I SEE THE BEAUTY
Of a sunset's glory,
Amazing artistry
Across the evening sky;
When I feel the mystery
Of a distant galaxy,
It awes and humbles me
To be loved by a God so high.

What can I do but thank You?
What can I do but give my life to You?
Hallelujah, hallelujah.
What can I do but praise You?
Every day make everything I do
A hallelujah, hallelujah,
Hallelujah.

When I hear the story
Of a God of mercy
Who shared humanity
And suffered by our side;
Of the cross they nailed You to
That could not hold You,
Now You're making all things new
By the power of Your risen life.

2132

Mark & Helen Johnson

WHEN I THINK ABOUT THE CROSS,
When I think of Jesus,
I'm reminded of His love –
Love that never leaves me.

Who am I that He should die,
Giving life so freely?
When I think about the cross,
Help me to believe it.

2133

Geraldine Latty & busbee

WHEN THE DAY BEGINS,
Let the morning bring
Mercy melodies that feed my soul.
When the evening comes
And the day is done,
Father, quiet me with songs of love.

So I can know You,
Hear what You say;
So I can walk with You
To the places that need Your grace.

In my hopes and dreams,
In everything I see,
Your perception is the truth I need.
In the things I do,
All that I pursue,
Thread Your presence
Through the heart of me.

Lord, I often trust
In what I see and what I touch.
Let my choices rest
In everything You are.

2134

Brian Houston

WHEN THE WAY AHEAD IS NOT CLEAR
And inspiration's not here;
When I'm in a dry and desert place
And I wanna see You face to face:

I don't wanna worship from afar,
I don't wanna follow foreign gods,
And if to worship is to kiss,
I won't settle for any less than this.

Could You look into my eyes tonight?
Could You purify my mind tonight?
Could You come and change my life tonight, Jesus?
If I worship You because You are Lord,
You sketched the heavens
And created the world,
And called my name
Before the day I was born,
Jesus, You're my Lord.

When the scriptures feel so dead to me
And I don't feel like I've been set free;
When all around they sing of victory,
But it's only darkness that I see:

2135

Keith & Kristyn Getty

WHEN TRIALS COME, no longer fear,
For in the pain our God draws near,
To fire a faith worth more than gold;
And there His faithfulness is told,
And there His faithfulness is told.

Within the night, I know Your peace;
The breath of God brings strength to me.
And new each morning mercy flows,
As treasures of the darkness grow,
As treasures of the darkness grow.

I turn to wisdom not my own,
For every battle You have known.
My confidence will rest in You;
Your love endures, Your ways are good,
Your love endures, Your ways are good.

When I am weary with the cost,
I see the triumph of the cross;
So in its shadow I shall run,
Till He completes the work begun,
Till He completes the work begun.

One day all things will be made new;
I'll see the hope You called me to.
And in Your kingdom paved with gold
I'll praise Your faithfulness of old,
I'll praise Your faithfulness of old.

2136

Lex Buckley

WHEN TROUBLE COMES
And you feel all alone;
When it is dark
And you cannot see ahead:

Hope in the Saviour of the world.
Put your trust
In the One who gave Himself,
For He lives and He reigns
On high over all.

Don't be afraid,
For the Father holds you close;
You're in His hands
And He will not let you go.

He won't let you go,
He won't let you go.
(Repeat)

2137

David Crowder

WHEN WE SING, hear our songs to You.
When we dance, feel us move to You.
When we laugh, fill our smiles with You.

When we lift our voices louder still,
Can You hear us, can You feel?

We love You, Lord,
We love You, we love You.
We love You, Lord,
We love You, we love You.

When we sing loud, hear our songs to You.
When we dance round, feel us move to You.
When we laugh aloud, fill our smiles with You.

And our love is big, our love is loud;
Fill this place with this love now.
And our love is big, our love is loud;
Fill this place with this love now.

(Second time)
Fill our lungs to sing it now.

We lift our voices louder still;
Our God is near, our God is here.

2138

Mark Beswick & Howard Francis

WHERE DO I GO when I'm feeling down?
Who do I call when friends aren't around?
I look to the lifter of my head,
Jesus, my Saviour, Lord and friend.

He will not suffer my foot to be moved;
The One who keeps me will watch over you.
Trust in the Lord, believe, have faith,
Lift up your voice to Him and say:

'I will lift up mine eyes to the hills
From whence cometh my strength;
My help cometh from the Lord,
Who made heaven and earth.'

2139

Paul & Lex Buckley

WHERE IS THE LOVE I once knew?
Why has my passion faded?
I search for You, Lord Jesus,
But You stay hidden.

Where is the song in my heart?
Where are the dreams I once dreamt?
I listen for Your voice, Lord,
But You stay silent.

O Lord, have mercy on me,
Open these ears to hear
And these eyes to see.
How I've longed for Your presence.
Just to draw near to You,
Jesus, is all that I want.

2140

Godfrey & Gill Birtill, Geraldine Latty & Tim Lomax

WHERE, OH WHERE'S YOUR PRESENCE, O GOD,
In this dry and weary land?
So many people drifting away.
How we need to understand:
You're still God,
Even when we're unbelieving;
Still God,
When we're desperate for our healing;
Still God, still God, still God.
You're still God,
Even when our friends desert us;
Still God,
Even through the things that hurt us;
Still God, still God.
So I will be still and know You are God.

Where, oh where's Your kingdom, O God?
We have let holiness go.
So many idols litter our land.
We've got to let this nation know:
You're still God,
When the government has no answers;
Still God,
When the media lowers the standard;
Still God, still God, still God.
You're still God,
When the plans we make are worthless;
Still God,
When we lose our sense of purpose;
Still God, still God.
So I will be still and know You are God.

When will Jesus really be seen
Through the church that bears His name?
Agents of His kingdom, His peace,
In the world for which he came.

You're still God,
Even though You were rejected;
Still God,
Though You were ridiculed, deserted;
Still God, still God, still God.
You're still God,
Though You suffered execution;
Still God,
You're alive and Christ our champion;
Still God, still God.
So I will be still and know You are God.

2141

Nick Herbert & Matt Redman

WHERE THE MORNING DAWNS and the evening fades,
We will make Your praise so glorious.
Let the awesome sound of Your song be heard
Here on earth just like in heaven.

Nothing in this world could stop us
Celebrating Your name, Jesus.

Nothing can stand
In the way of Your song:
Holy are You, Lord; holy are You, Lord.
For now and forever
Your praise will be sung:
Holy are You, Lord; holy are You, Lord God.

Every time we meet we will celebrate,
Make Your praise a great occasion.
We open wide the doors, call the nations in
To the glory of Your kingdom.

2142

Andy Smith

WHO CAN DESCRIBE YOU TO ME?
You are such a mystery.
Greater things no one has seen.
And I've found that oh,
I love You so.

Jesus, Redeemer,
You are the Prince of Peace.
My strong deliverer,
You gave Your life for me.
I've found that oh,
I love You so.

You are the same yesterday,
Today and forever more,
Yet You chose to lay Yourself down.
And I've found that oh,
I love You so.

2143

Martyn Layzell

WHO CAN KNOW the mind of our Creator?
Who can speak of wonders yet unseen?
Who can reach the height of understanding,
To play the notes of wisdom's melody?

Who has weighed the dust of every mountain?
Who has walked the mysteries of the deep?
Who has laid the earth on its foundation
And who conducts the waves upon the sea?

I stand in awe of You,
I stand in awe of You,
So glorious and true:
I stand in awe,
I stand in awe.

You have seen the end from the beginning.
You have been before the world began.
You have reached to me within my darkness,
And in the light of mercy now I see.

2144

Noel Richards

WHO CAN MEND HEARTS THAT ARE BROKEN?
Who can bring comfort to all those who mourn?
Who can bring light in the darkest times?
Who can bring peace to the fearful mind?

We have the answer, treasure to share;
Through our endeavour
God's love is declared.
We have the answer,
Through us He brings good news
To all the world!

Who can bring strength to those who faint?
Who can bring healing to all those in pain?
Who can bring hope that removes despair?
Who can bring friendship when nobody cares?

Who took the blame for our shameful ways?
Who mends the damage of our wasted years?
Who gives the guilty a second chance?
Who sets us free from the grip of the past?

All humankind soon will hear of God;
Millions are ready to speak of His love.
He sends His Spirit upon the church
To take His good news throughout the world.

2145

Matt Redman & Paul Baloche

WHO COULD IMAGINE A MELODY
True enough to tell of Your mercy?
Who could imagine a harmony
Sweet enough to tell of Your love?

I see the heavens proclaiming You
Day after day,
And I know in my heart
That there must be a way:

To sing a greater song,
A greater song to You on the earth;
To sing a greater song,
A greater song to You on the earth.

Who could imagine a symphony
Grand enough to tell of Your glory?
Our highest praise but a feeble breath,
A whisper of Your thunderous worth.

Hallelujah,
We wanna lift You higher.
(Repeat)
Higher, higher.

2146

Keith & Kristyn Getty

WHO HEARS,
Who hears the voice of the hungry, the thirsty?
Who sees,
Who sees the tears of the suffering ones?

Imagine a King who would come
Through the darkness
And walk where I walk,

Full of greatness,
And call me to His side,
Just like a father and child.

Who knows,
Who knows the hopes that lie hidden, forgotten?
Who comes,
Who comes to lead all the children home?

2147

Paul Baloche

WHO IS LIKE HIM,
The Lion and the Lamb
Seated on the throne?
Mountains bow down,
Every ocean roars
To the Lord of hosts.

Praise Adonai,
From the rising of the sun
Till the end of every day.
Praise Adonai,
All the nations of the earth
And the angels and the saints
Sing praise.

2148

Geraldine Latty & busbee

WHO IS LIKE THE LORD our God,
Moving in our lives with surprising love?
We thought the lion would overthrow,
But saw the Lamb through suffering go.

God, whose strength holds the universe,
Came to live with us,
Chose to die our death.
We thought that we would pay the price;
Discovered that You gave Your life.

You are the song of yesterday,
You are the anthem of today.
You're the beginning and the end,
The only way.
Who can define Your tenderness,
Limit the passion of Your grace?
You're magnificent in all Your ways.

Holy and surprising God,
Powerful in truth,
Vulnerable in love.
Your sacrifice will one day be
The song that fills eternity.

Holy is the Lamb of God,
Holy is our Saviour;
Awesome power and surprising love,
We are Yours forever.

2149

Noel Robinson & Sam Blake

WHY DO YOU WAIT?
Receive Him today;
He is waiting to answer your call.
He can heal your broken heart today,
So come, oh come, oh come.
(Repeat)

Jesus is waiting, Jesus is waiting,
Jesus is waiting to answer your call.
(Repeat)

2150

Martyn Layzell & busbee

WITH ALL MY HEART I say I love You.
And it's my reward to stand before You.
With all my heart, *(echo)*
With all my soul, *(echo)*
With all my strength I worship You.

You are my heart's desire;
Nothing compares to You.
Jesus, my one desire,
I worship You.
Passionate hearts on fire
Sing in this place for You,
Bowing before Your throne
To honour You.

The life I live I'm living for You,
With every breath I say I love You.
With all my heart, *(echo)*
With all my soul, *(echo)*
With all my strength I worship You.

Every nation, all of creation,
Every heart will sing Your praise.
With celebration, songs of salvation
Bless Your name.
Every nation, all of creation,
Every heart will sing Your praise.
With celebration, songs of salvation
We proclaim.

2151

Nathan Fellingham

WONDERFUL LORD,
So full of grace,
So full of mercy.

Mighty You are,
With power to save,
Power to heal.
And I will worship You,
I give my life to You.

You are faithful to me
And will never cease to be;
All Your promises will come to pass
In Your power and sovereignty.
You are faithful and true,
Perfect timing in all You do.
So I'll never stop trusting You;
You are God and You are good,
So good to me.

Great is Your love,
You lift up my head
When darkness surrounds me.
Tender You are,
Holding me close,
You never let go.
And I will worship You,
I give my life to You.

2152

Doug Horley

WONDERFUL LORD, wonderful God,
You are my shield, my protector.
I can lie down, go off to sleep,
Knowing You're watching over me.
Wonderful Lord, wonderful God,
Help me to trust You forever.
I need not fear, 'cause You are near,
I can lie down and sleep in peace.

2153

Mark Beswick & Howard Francis

WONDERFUL, YOU ARE
Wonderful, You are
Wonderful.

Marvellous . . .

Glorious . . .

Beautiful . . .

Excellent . . .

Prince of Peace . . .

Lord of all . . .

King of kings . . .

Mighty God . . .

2154

Geraldine Latty & busbee

WORSHIP GOD WITH THE MORNING SUNRISE,
Lift your voice in the evening rain.
Bring your thanks and praise,
All your accolades to Him.
Clap your hands to the God who loves us.
Sing your song to the One who saves.
Trust His promises,
Know that we are His always!

You are beautifully different,
You are gracious in Your thoughts.
You're the friend who's proven faithful,
You are love laid down for us.

We are caught up in Your beauty,
We are always in Your thoughts.
Even in our disappointments,
We are known and we are loved.

We have come to give You praise,
We have come to bless Your name.
We will always be amazed
At how You love us.
(Repeat)

2155

Al Gordon

WORSHIP THE LORD in the beauty of holiness;
With awe and with reverence, bow to adore.
You are my Lord, You are my holiness,
Jesus, my righteousness, I worship You, Lord.

I'm living for Your glory,
I'm living for the Name above all names.
No one else is worthy,
No one else can ever take Your place.

I worship You, Lord, in beautiful holiness;
Lifting up reverence, I bow to adore.
I give You my all, surrendering everything;
My everyday offering, to worship You, Lord.

You are high and lifted up,
High and lifted up,
High and lifted up.
(Repeat)

2156

Johnny Parks & Phil Mawhinney

YOU ARE JUSTICE
That never ends –
That's who You are.

You're a river
That never fails –
Of righteousness.

Freedom, not religion,
Is what You want.

I won't ignore
Your words, O God;
As I respond
Transform my heart.

At times my worship
And offering
Are empty, Lord.
You're the God who gives me
A second chance.
Transform me now.

Freedom, not religion,
Compassion, not just words,
Love beyond these walls
Is what You want.

You're the God who gives us
A second chance.
(Repeat)

2157

Nick Herbert & Tim Hughes

YOU ARE MORE THAN HEARTS COULD EVER IMAGINE,
Than minds could ever conceive;
There's always more to discover
Of You.

You reveal Yourself to those who are searching,
To those who sit at Your feet;
Jesus, You'll find us waiting
On our knees.

You're glorious, so glorious;
King of love, let Your light shine brightly.
You're everything we're hoping for.
Our one desire is to see Your glory.

Gracious One, lead us into Your presence
As we lift up Your name.
Jesus, come down and touch the earth again.

Could we see Your glory?
Could we see Your glory?
Could we see Your glory
Here on earth, O Lord?

Could we taste Your glory?
Could we taste Your glory?
Could we taste Your glory
Here on earth?

2158

Noel & Michelle-John Robinson

YOU ARE MY HEALER in time of trouble.
When You show up strong,
I overcome.

Yeah, yeah, yeah.

You're my healer in trouble;
You're my healer, You are, You are.
Yeah, yeah, yeah,
Yeah, yeah, You are, You are.

2159

Andy Bromley

YOU ARE NEAR,
Behind and before.
You laid Your hand upon me,

Too wonderful to know.
You are near,
Always by my side.
Unfailing love surrounds me,
I trust in You alone.
So where can I go from You?
If I go to the heights, You are there.
Lie down in the depths, You are there.
You're everywhere.

You are near,
Even though I cannot see You.
Sometimes I cannot feel You.
Still I know You've promised
You are near,
Even through the deepest valley.
Sometimes the night surrounds me –
Even there Your hand will guide me,
Even there Your hand will hold me.

(Second time)
Even there Your light will shine on me.

There's nowhere you can go
That He won't be,
Nothing you can do
That He won't see.
There's nothing you can say
That He won't hear,
Nowhere you can hide
That He won't find.
Your deepest thoughts,
Your deepest needs,
He knows them all,
He sees all things,
And still He loves and still He holds
And still He gives.
And still He loves and still He holds
And still He gives.

2160

Darlene Zschech

YOU ARE RIGHTEOUS,
You love justice,
And those who honour You
Will see Your face.
I will arise
And lift my eyes
To see Your majesty, Your holiness,
And all I am will bless You.

My hope is in the name of the Lord,
Where my help comes from;
You're my strength, my song.
My trust is in the name of the Lord;
I will sing Your praise,
You are faithful.

2161

Simon Goodall

YOU ARE SO BEAUTIFUL,
You are so lovely;
You are so wonderful,
My King of love.

Jesus, You're all I need,
You are the air I breathe.
My soul, it longs for You;
Jesus, I love You.

2162

Paul Oakley & Chris Spring

YOU ARE SO GOOD TO ME;
I did not know You,
But I heard You call out my name.

I couldn't see You,
But I felt You reach into my heart,
Take all my fear and shame,
Pour all Your kindness in –
You turned my life around.
And now You have opened up my eyes
To the mystery of Your grace.

I could sing, I could dance in the street,
I could shout from the roof
How Your love set me free,
How this gospel is true.
You're the way, You're the truth, You're the life,
And I will always follow You,
You make all things new.
Jesus, You are good.

You are like no one else;
You reign forever, Jesus.
Name above every name,
Today, forever, You're the same.
You conquered sin for me,
Your blood has made me clean.
Your mercy covers me,
Your goodness leads me on.
And now I can never be the same;
You alone deserve my praise.

There is only one way,
There is only one name,
There is only one God.
Jesus, You, and You alone, can save.

2163

Chris Tomlin, Ed Cash, Matt Redman, Jesse Reeves &
Daniel Carson

YOU ARE THE FIRST,
You go before;
You are the last,
Lord, You're the encore.
Your name's in lights
For all to see;
The starry host
Declare Your glory.

Glory in the highest,
Glory in the highest,
Glory in the highest.

Apart from You
There is no God,
Light of the world,
The bright and morning star.
Your name will shine
For all to see;
You are the One,
You are my glory.

And no one else could ever compare
To You, Lord.
All the earth together declare:
Glory in the highest,
Glory in the highest,
Glory in the highest
To You, Lord.

All the earth will sing Your praise –
The moon and stars, the sun and rain.
Every nation will proclaim
That You are God and You will reign.

Glory, glory, hallelujah.
Glory, glory to You, Lord.
Glory, glory, hallelujah.
Hallelujah.

2164

Simon Brading

YOU ARE THE ROCK on which I stand;
All that surrounds is sinking sand.
Days of darkness may shadow my path,
But I know I'm held in Your hand.

Seasons will change, but You remain,
Even through drought and tears of pain.
Safe within Your truth I'll stay,
For I'm Yours, I'm held in Your hand.

I'll sing through tears and the smiles.
I'll sing through rain or shine.
I'll sing of unending grace.
I'll sing just to give You praise, my Lord.

All earthly things will fade away;
Your promises, Lord, remain the same.
Trials may come from day to day;
Still, I know I'm held in Your hand.

A time will come when suffering will end,
But until that day
You won't abandon me.
Forever I'll stand, held in Your hand.

2165

Keith & Kristyn Getty

YOU ARE THE SHEPHERD,
I belong to You.
When I walk on rough ground,

You can guide me through.
You know my name,
You know my voice.
Before I was born,
I was Your choice.
Show me how to follow;
Lord, keep me close to You.
You are the Shepherd,
I belong to You.

Open eyes to see You are the way.
Open ears to hear You are the truth.
Open hearts to know You are the Lord of life.
For every land You hold a special plan.

2166

David Gate

YOU ARE THE SHOUT OF THE NATIONS,
You are the angels' song.
You are the sound of creation, Jesus,
We bow before Your throne
To bring You praise,
Bring You praise.

For I was made to worship You,
To serve You every day.
Lord, I was made for Your delight,
To bless Your heart,
To bring You praise.

You are the source of all good things,
You are the author of life.
You are the end and beginning, Jesus;
We bow to lift You high
And bring You praise,
Bring You praise.

2167

Matt Crocker

YOU BOUGHT MY LIFE

With the blood You shed on the cross
When You died for the sins of men,
And You let out a cry,
Crucified, now alive in me.

These hands are Yours.
Teach them to serve as You please,
And I'll reach out,
Desperate to see all the greatness of God.
May my soul rest assured in You.
I'll never be the same;
No, I'll never be the same.

'Cause I know that You're alive,
You came to fix my broken life.
And I sing to glorify
Your holy name, Jesus Christ.

You've changed it all.
You broke down the wall when I spoke
And confessed,
In You I'm blessed, now I walk in the light,
In victorious sight of You.
I'll never be the same;
No, I'll never be the same.

Your fire fall down,
Fire fall down on us, we pray.
As we seek, Your fire fall down,
Fire fall down on us, we pray.
(Repeat)

Show me Your heart,
Show me Your way,
Show me Your glory.
(Repeat)

2168

Vicky Beeching

YOU CAN SHINE LIGHT into the darkness
And You can set every prisoner free.
And You can make streams flow in the desert,
And this is what we are longing to see.
Because we know and we believe:

Nothing, nothing is impossible for You.
Anything, anything can happen
When Your power breaks through.
Hear our cry for Your supernatural touch.
God of miracles, come and visit us.

Come, Lord, shine light into the darkness.
Come, Lord, set every prisoner free.
Come, Lord, make streams flow in the desert,
'Cause this is the time we are longing to see.
Because we know and we believe:

2169

Nathan Fellingham

YOU DID NOT CONSIDER
Using all Your strength and power
To gain Yourself an earthly crown;
But instead You suffered,
Pouring out Your life for us
To reconcile us back to God.

What love You showed in doing this for us:
My heart, it overflows.

So I'm pouring out a song
Of love and adoration
To the One who's captivated
My attention: Jesus Christ,

The hero of mankind's salvation.
Thank You, Lord,
For this life You've won for me.

Death could not defeat You;
From the grave You rose again,
Ascending to Your Father's side.
Then You sent the Spirit,
Your power now at work in us,
To demonstrate Your truth and light.

Jesus, I will follow You,
Live each day consecrated to Your will.
Then one day You will return
And I'll know perfect joy forever more.

2170

Vicky Beeching

YOU FORMED US FROM THE DUST,
You breathed Your breath in us;
We are the work of Your hands.
Now we breathe back to You
Love songs of gratitude,
Adoring You with all we have.

We were created
To worship Your name,
And we were created
To bring You our praise.

(Second time)
So we will worship,
So we will praise
You, our Creator,
For all our days.

If we don't worship You,
We'll search for substitutes
To fill the void in our hearts.
Worshipping other things
Destroys our liberty,
But as we praise You, we are free.

For this is what we were made to do. *(x3)*
So we lift up our praise to You.

2171

Nathan & Lou Fellingham & busbee

YOU GIVE REST to the weary,
You bring strength to the weak;
As they wait in Your presence,
There is grace for their need.
So I'll wait, I'll wait;
Yes, I'll wait, I'll wait for You.

I will say of the Lord, 'He is my refuge.'
I will say of the Lord, 'He is my strength.'
I will say of the Lord, 'He is my shelter,
My hiding place.'
I will come to the source of all creation;
I will drink from the well that never dries.
I will draw from the One who won't grow tired,
The Lord of all.

You can come in the silence;
You can come in the noise.
Bringing peace in a moment,
Bringing comfort and joy.
So I'll wait, I'll wait;
Yes, I'll wait, I'll wait for You.

2172

YOU HAVE LOVED ME with such perfect love,
Fathered me with such a tender touch.
Your faithfulness surrounds my soul,
Your mercy lifts my head.
How could I repay all You have done?

Father me, faithful Father.
Father me;
No one else could ever be
The perfect Father God to me.

You now clothe me with Your righteousness,
Hide me in the shadow of Your wings.
And even in my darkest days,
Your light will guide my way.
Hallelujah to the King of grace.

2173

YOU HAVE MY HEART
And I am Yours forever.
You are my strength,
God of grace and power.

And everything
You hold in Your hand;
Still You make time for me –
I can't understand.

Praise You, God of earth and sky.
How beautiful is Your unfailing love,
Unfailing love.

And You never change, God,
You remain the holy One
And my unfailing love,
Unfailing love.

You are my rock,
The One I hold on to.
You are my song
And I sing for You.

2174

Gareth Robinson

YOU HAVE PROMISED to be with us
As we go out seeking first Your kingdom,
As we hold out Your light that shines in darkness,
As we speak Your words of loving kindness.
Jesus, You have promised
And we trust Your faithful word.

We will go in peace
To love and serve the Lord,
In the name of Christ, amen.

You have promised heaven's power
As we tell of life in all its fullness,
As we follow Your call to make disciples
In the name of the Father, Son and Spirit.
Jesus, You have promised
And we trust Your faithful word.

Where there is pain, bring healing.
Where there's despair, bring hope.
Bringing Your joy in sadness,
Bringing Your love to all.

2175

Darlene Zschech

YOU HOLD IT ALL AT ONCE,
The earth and all within;
You look with eyes of love
To the sons of man.
That I am known by You
Compels my heart to sing:

I live to know You more,
I live to know You more.
I live to know You more,
For me to live is Christ;
To know You is my life.

The storms will come and go,
There's laughter and there's pain;
Your kindness leads me on
To the light again.
So I live and breathe,
And find myself in You.

I live to know You,
I live to know You,
I live to know You more.

I count it all but loss,
Compared to knowing You.
I give my life away
To know You any day.

2176

Vicky Beeching & Marc Byrd

YOU KNOW ME COMPLETELY
Like no other could.
You love me so freely

When no other would.
Your love's a mystery:
For all eternity I'll be with You.

You have won my heart forever more.
You are mine and I'm forever Yours.
You are my desire, my treasure in this life,
And You have won my heart
forever more.

One day I will see You,
Standing face to face.
One day I'll run into
My Saviour's strong embrace.
It's such a mystery.
For all eternity, I'll be with You.

Jesus, how I love You.
Jesus, how I love You.
My heart is Yours, forever more.

2177

Charlie Hall & Matt Redman

YOU PART THE HEAVENS,
Touch the earth,
You open eyes to see Your worth;
And the walls are coming down,
And the walls are coming down.
And every plan of Yours prevails,
Lord, Your purpose never fails;
And the walls are coming down,
Yes, the walls are coming down,
And the walls are falling now.

With a hand of strength
And a heart of grace,
You are merciful

And mighty to save.
So pour Your power out,
Let a rising shout
Echo through the earth
As Your kingdom comes;
Let Your kingdom come.

We are marked here by Your power,
We are ready for this hour;
And the walls are coming down,
Yes, the walls are coming down.
You are building up Your bride,
You are filling her with fire;
And the walls are coming down,
Yes, the walls are coming down,
And the walls are falling now.

And the clouds are blowing now,
And Your truth is raining down.
And the earth is shaking now
With the thunder of Your power.
And the walls are coming down,
Yes, the walls are coming down.
There's a shout that's rising now.

2178

Matt Redman
Chorus: Robert Lowry (1826–1899)/Matt Redman

YOUR BLOOD SPEAKS A BETTER WORD
Than all the empty claims
I've heard upon this earth;
Speaks righteousness for me
And stands in my defence.
And Jesus, it's Your blood.

Your cross testifies in grace,
Tells of the Father's heart
To make a way for us.

Now boldly we approach,
Not by earthly confidence,
It's only by Your blood.

What can wash away our sins?
What can make us whole again?
Nothing but the blood,
Nothing but the blood of Jesus.
What can wash us pure as snow,
Welcomed as the friends of God?
Nothing but the blood,
Nothing but Your blood, King Jesus.

2179

Andy Smith

YOU'RE MIGHTY AND POWERFUL TO SAVE.
My feet bare, my fear for You displayed.
You touch me and disintegrate my blame;
I'll never be the same.
And our faces now uncovered
Reveal the awesome glory of Your Son.
Will You put Your voice within me,
So they can hear the sweet song that You sing?
Salvation song.

Your sunrise on a darkened land;
Long shadows, by noon nowhere to stand.
The lost come – by Your blood they are redeemed;
Together we will sing
That we love You, O King Jesus,
Forever You're the lover of my soul.
As Your presence falls upon us,
Your glory now revealed.
And God, we pray Your song will fill our land:
Salvation song.

2180

Nick Herbert & Matt Redman

YOU'RE PRAISEWORTHY, *so praiseworthy,*
Jesus, Saviour, King forever.
Blessing, honour, wisdom, power
Be to You for now and ever.

For the cross and for the crown,
For the thorns and for the throne,
That in mercy You came down.

In the calm and in the storm,
For Your peace and for Your power,
Ever present, ever strong.

Hallelujah, hallelujah,
You're praiseworthy, so praiseworthy.

2181

Evan Rogers

YOU'RE THE FIRST and You're the last;
Everything is at Your command.
You are immortal, invisible,
The King eternal,
The only wise God.
You've got everything at Your feet;
You have crushed the enemy.
You are the mighty conqueror,
Strong deliverer.
To You we'll bow our knees.

You reign supreme,
You are the Lord, the King of kings.
You reign supreme
Above all powers and authorities.
You reign supreme

Over all created things.
You reign supreme,
Lord, You reign over me.

Jesus, You will own all praise;
No one else can share Your fame.
You are highly exalted,
Glorious, victorious,
The Name above all names.
You've got my whole life in Your hands,
All my dreams and all my plans.
You're my righteous Redeemer,
Sovereign Saviour.
In my heart You will reign.

Yes, You rule,
You rule and You reign.
(Repeat)

2182

Mark Beswick, Howard Francis, Noel Robinson,
Priscilla Mae Campbell & Laurine Cato

YOU'RE THE MIGHTY GOD;
We adore You,
We love to sing Your praises
All day long.
You're the mighty God;
Everybody lift up His holy name,
Lift His holy name.

Jesus, wonderful name;
Jesus, to You belong the praise and glory.
Jesus, mighty to save;
Let heaven and earth proclaim.

What a mighty God;
Give Him glory, glory.
What a mighty God;

Let's celebrate.
Oh, what a mighty God;
Give Him glory, glory.
What a mighty God;
We give to You the praise.

2183

Andy Smith

YOU'RE THE ONE, the holy King;
I trust in You for everything.
I boast in You, You're all I need,
And I believe we're gonna see
The goodness of the Lord.
(Repeat)

I want to belong
To a generation that is strong.
Laying hold of Your kingdom,
We prophesy to the breath:
Let the army arise.

We will fight and we will run
Headlong into the battle till it's won.
Your name's renown is what we raise;
Jesus, come and take Your place.

You call us now to higher things,
To live a life of love for You;
Unity is what we need,
So let the church arise
And see the glory of the Lord.

Your promises are gonna be,
'Cause idle words You do not speak.
Streams of life flow unrestrained.
You're gonna move like we've never seen.
The lost will be redeemed.

2184

Marty Sampson

YOUR FAITHFUL LOVE
Has always been there for me –
The greatest love that I have ever known.
What can I give to You
For all You've given to me?
You gave it all
And You are all I need.

You are my King,
You are my God.
The praises I bring
Come from my heart.

This is for You,
For all You've done for me,
And I wanted to show You
How much You mean, my God,
My God.

2185

Matt Maher

YOUR GRACE IS POWER,
Your will forever.
Your love is a river;
Overflow in me.

Your word, true presence.
Your body, our recompense.
Your blood, salvation;
Overflow in me.

Overflow in me, my Lord.
Overflow in me, my Lord.
Let Your people bless You

As Your cup is poured;
Overflow in me, my Lord.
Overflow in me, my Lord.

Your worship of You,
It's Your gift to us from You.
No one could give this gift but You;
Overflow in me.

We lift up our hearts,
We lift up our souls,
We lift up our minds,
And every good thing is Yours.
Yeah, every good thing is Yours,
So overflow.

2186

Lex Buckley

YOUR HEART IS FOR THE BROKEN,
Your ears are turned to those in pain.
You comfort all in mourning,
You rescue those in need.

So though I walk through the valley,
I won't be afraid,
For Jesus, You are with me,
Holding me close.
And You can give a peace
That passes understanding.
Lord, You will protect
And comfort this heart.

Lord, I know You are faithful.
Lord, I know You are good and true.
I trust in You, my Saviour;
You are my all in all.

O Lord, all of my hope is in You,
All of my hope is in You.
All of my hope is in You,
It's in You.

2187

Vicky Beeching

YOUR LAUGHTER,
It echoes like a joyous thunder.
Your whisper,
It warms me like a summer breeze.
Your anger is fiercer
Than the sun in its splendour.
You're close and yet full of mystery.
Ever since the day that I saw Your face,
Try as I may I cannot look away,
I cannot look away.

Captivated by You,
I am captivated by You.
May my life be one unbroken gaze,
Fixed upon the beauty of Your face.

Beholding is becoming,
So as You fill my gaze,
I become more like You
And my heart is changed.
Beholding is becoming,
So as You fill my view,
Transform me into the likeness of You.
This is what I ask for all my days:
That I may never look away,
Never look away.

Captivated by You,
I am captivated by You.
May my life be one unbroken gaze,
Fixed upon Your beauty,
Fixed upon Your beauty.

No other could ever be as beautiful.
No other could ever steal my heart away.
(Repeat)
I just can't look away.

2188

Raymond Badham

YOUR LIGHT IS OVER ME,
Flooding over me;
The night is lifted.
Heaven over me,
Flooding over me;
I can't contain it.
My cup overflows.
My cup overflows.

Praise the Lord with all my heart.
Praise Him for He has done great things.
His banner over me
Is love, His love;
His banner over me
Is love, His love.

You brought the sunshine in
And turned the dark to day.
You made the shadows flee away.
You opened up my eyes
To a new and living way,
The dawning of a brand new day.

2189

Reuben Morgan

YOUR LOVE, O LORD, IS LIKE THE OCEANS,
Deeper than endless seas.
Your faithfulness is like the mountains,
And Your word never fails.

Glory to God, let every heart sing:
Glory to God in the highest.
Let us adore, wonderful Saviour;
Crown Him forever our King.

2190

Ben Fielding

YOUR LOVE REACHES OUT TO ME,
Your grace has made a way to You,
Made a way to You.
Your word lives inside of me,
Your truth is life to all who hear,
Life to all who hear.

We live for You,
Live Your truth.

May Your kingdom come
And Your will be done
As we serve Your heart,
Serve Your heart.
Let salvation flow
As Your people pray:
Lord, we long for more,
Long for more.

In You death is overcome,
No power can stand against Your name,
The power of Your name.

In faith we will rise to be
Your hands and feet to all the earth,
Life to all the earth.

2191

Matt Redman

YOUR MERCY TAUGHT US HOW TO DANCE,
To celebrate with all we have,
And we'll dance to thank You for mercy.
Your glory taught us how to shout.
We'll lift Your name in all the earth
And we'll shout to the praise of Your glory.

It's the overflow of a forgiven soul.
And now we've seen You, God,
Our hearts cannot stay silent.

And we'll be a dancing generation,
Dancing because of Your great mercy, Lord,
Your great mercy, Lord.
And we'll be a shouting generation,
Shouting because of Your great glory, Lord,
Your great glory, Lord.

2192

Tim Hughes

YOUR NAME IS HIGHLY EXALTED;
Jesus, forever be glorified,
Forever be glorified.
Your name has power to conquer;
Your fame resounds throughout heaven and earth,
Resounds throughout heaven and earth.

Name above all names,
You are glorious,
Wonderful and true;

Powerful are You.
There will be a day
When every knee will bow
Before Your holiness,
Every tongue confess,
Name above all names.

Rulers will one day be silent,
Lost in the wonder and awe of Your name,
The wonder and awe of Your name.
Eternal, none is Your equal.
We cry: 'No other god but You,
No other god but You.'

Every knee must bow,
Every knee must bow,
Every knee must bow to You.
(Repeat)

2193

Andy Bromley

YOUR NAME, STRONGER THAN I KNOW,
Deeper than a thousand words could say,
Your name.
Your name, fire in my soul,
Healing for a hurting heart today,
Your name, Your name.
And my heart will bow and my spirit soar,
And my soul cries out to the Lord of all.
To my God and King, to my Prince of Peace,
I will lift my voice in praise
Unto Your name, unto Your name.

Your name, all creation knows
The One who gave it life with breath alone,
Your name.
Your name, glory now displayed;

All the earth belongs to You alone,
Your name, Your name.
And the mountains bow, and the seas will roar,
And the rocks cry out, all creation calls.
To the holy One, to the Son of God
We will lift our voice in praise:
Worship Your name, worship Your name.

Your name, higher than them all;
Holy One of God, the Lord of lords,
Your name.
Your name, heaven's only Son,
High and lifted up forever more,
Your name, Your name.
And the nations bow and their kingdoms fall;
Every king and priest, every prince and lord,
Falling to their knees will acknowledge You.
We will lift our voice in praise:
Honour Your name, honour Your name.

2194

Joel Houston

YOURS IS THE KINGDOM
And the power,
And the glory forever is Yours;
Heaven and earth bow down
In the wonder of Your name.
Heaven is open,
Death is broken,
And the glory forever is Yours;
Nothing can overcome
The power of Your name.

King above kings,
All the universe will sing,
Everlasting God,
You are wonderful,
You are wonderful.

And the shout of the earth
Will be Your praise,
God, forever.
And the light unto all
Will be Your wonderful name.
For the glory, Lord, is Yours.
God, forever
All the glory, Lord, is Yours.

2195

Tim Hughes & John G. Whittier (1807–1892)

YOUR VOICE HAS STILLED the raging storms;
The wind and waves bow down before.
Your still, small voice brings hope to all
Who wait on You.
We'll wait for You
To lead us to the place
Where You'll restore our souls,
And all our earthly strivings come to cease.

Take from our souls the strain and stress,
And let our ordered lives confess
The beauty of Your peace,
The beauty of Your peace.

Bright skies will soon be overhead;
We'll enter into heaven's rest.
There'll be no death, there'll be no pain;
The things of old will pass away.
You'll lead us to the place
Where You'll restore our souls,
And all our earthly strivings come to cease.

2196

David Gate

YOUR VOICE IS LIKE THUNDER,
Like the roar of the sea.
Yet You talk to us in whispers,
And You sing songs over me.

Intimately yet reverently
You call us, call us to praise.
(Repeat)

Your hands craft rivers and mountains,
And they hold stars in their place.
Yet still Your arms are open,
Our hearts You freely embrace.

With my face on the ground,
My heart bowing down,
What else can I do
But fall down and worship You?
(Repeat)

2197

Chris Bowater

YOUR WORD:
Truth unchanged, unchanging,
Constant firm foundation,
Steadfast and secure.
Your word:
Healing to the nations,
Light into the darkness,
Lamp unto my feet.

All that there is written remains
And ever shall be.
Life itself shall fade away;

Your word alone endures.
Living, energising Word,
Activate the people.
Revolutionise our lives
And in our hearts be sealed.

And in our hearts be hidden,
In our hearts be hidden,
And in our hearts be hidden.

2198

Brian Doerksen

YOU SHINE
Brighter than the brightest star;
Your love,
Purer than the purest heart.
You shine,
Filling us with courage and strength
To follow You.

Why should I fear man
When You made the heavens?
Why should I be afraid
When You put the stars in place?
Why should I lose heart
When I know how great You are?
Why should I give up
When Your plans are full of love?

In this world we will have trouble,
But You have overcome the world.

2199

Joel Houston

YOU STOOD BEFORE CREATION,
Eternity in Your hand;
You spoke the earth into motion,
My soul now to stand.

You stood before my failure
And carried the cross for my shame;
My sin weighed upon Your shoulders,
My soul now to stand.

So what can I say
And what could I do
But offer this heart, O God,
Completely to You?

I'll walk upon salvation,
Your Spirit alive in me;
This life to declare Your promise:
My soul now to stand.

So I'll stand with arms high and heart abandoned,
In awe of the One who gave it all.
I'll stand, my soul, Lord, to You surrendered;
All I am is Yours.

2200

Nathan Fellingham

YOU WERE THERE IN THE BEGINNING,
Jesus Christ, the Son of God.
With Your Father and the Spirit,
From nothing You made the universe.
You preserve all that You've made,
Giving life to all,
And the hosts of heaven worship You.

You are the Lord,
You made the heavens,
The highest heavens
And all the stars above.
You are the Lord,
You made the earth and sea
And every living thing
That lives beneath the sun.

Lord of all, You're highly exalted;
Who can compare to You, O God?
You're the author of creation's story,
And now it responds to worship You.
And Your power is displayed
As a sign to all,
And Your people stand in awe of You.

Addresses for Copyright and Information

Company names are under first name or word. Individuals' names are listed under surname.

Ambushed Ltd, 5–9 Surrey Street, Croydon, CR0 1RG, UK.
email: info@follysend.org
website: www.follysend.org

Ateliers et Presses de Taizé, F-71250 Taizé-Communauté, France.
email: community@taize.fr

Barrie, Karen, 511 Maple Ave., Wilmette, Illinois 60091, USA.

Barthow, Mary R., 15 Aunceston Rise, Alfriston, South Auckland, New Zealand.

Behrns, Gary, 2406 Colonial Hills Road, Jefferson City, MO 65109, USA.

Bucks Music Group Ltd, Onward House, 11 Uxbridge Street, London, W8 7TQ, UK. *(Rights administered in the UK & Republic of Ireland.)*

Central Board of Finance of the Church of England (The), Church House, Great Smith Street, London, SW1P 3NZ, UK.
email: copyright@c-of-e.org.uk

Chance, Kay, Dr. H.-Jasper-Str. 20, D-37581 Bad Gandersheim, Germany.

CopyCare, P.O. Box 77, Hailsham, East Sussex, BN27 3EF, UK.
email: music@copycare.com

Curious? Music UK, P.O. Box 40, Arundel, BN18 0UQ, UK.
email: info@furiousrecords.co.uk

Daniel L. Schutte & New Dawn Music, 5536 North East Hassalo, Portland, OR 97213, USA.

David Higham Associates Ltd, 5–8 Lower John Street, Golden Square, London, W1R 3PE, UK.

Daybreak Music Ltd, P.O. Box 2848, Eastbourne, BN20 7XP, UK.
email: info@daybreakmusic.co.uk

Dudley-Smith, Timothy, 9 Ashlands, Ford, Salisbury, SP4 6DY, UK. *(For Europe, incl. UK & Ireland, and in all territories not controlled by Hope Publishing Company.)*

GIA Publications Inc., 7404 South Mason Avenue, Chicago, IL 60638, USA.
website: www.giamusic.com

Gabriel Music Inc., P.O. Box 840999, Houston, Texas 77284-0999, USA.

Gordon V. Thompson, a division of Warner Chappell Music Canada Ltd, 40 Sheppard Avenue West, Suite 800, Toronto, Ontario, M2N 6K9, Canada.

Grace! Music, 11610 Grandview Road, Kansas City, MO 64137, USA.

Heart of David Music, 14815 Pineview Drive, Grandview, MO 64030, USA.

High-Fye Music Ltd, 8–9 Frith Street, London, W1D 3JB, UK. *(Used by permission of Music Sales Ltd.)*

IQ Music Ltd, Commercial House, 52 Perrymount Road, Haywards Heath, West Sussex, RH16 3DT, UK. *(For the world.)*
email: iqbal@iqmusic.co.uk

ICG, P.O. Box 24149, Nashville, TN 37202, USA.

Josef Weinberger Ltd, 12–14 Mortimer Street, London, W1N 7RD, UK.

Jubilate Hymns Ltd, Southwick House, 4 Thorne Park Road, Chelston, Torquay, TQ2 6RX, UK.
email: jubilatemw@aol.com

King, Mary Lou, 7013 E. Keynote, Longbeach, CA 90808, USA.

Kingdom Faith Ministries, Foundry Lane, Horsham, West Sussex, RH13 5PX, UK.

Kingswaysongs.com, P.O. Box 75, Eastbourne, East Sussex, BN23 6NW, UK.
email: tym@kingsway.co.uk

Lea, Melva, Larry Lea Ministries, P.O. Box 1102, Sherman, TX75091-1102, USA.

Len Magee Music, P.O. Box 6327, South Tweed Heads, NSW 2486, Australia.

MCA Music Publishing, 2440 Sepulveda Blvd Suite 100, Los Angeles, CA 90064-1712, USA. *(Used by permission of Music Sales Ltd.)*

Make Way Music, email: info@makewaymusic.com

McIntosh, Mike & Claire, P.O. Box 24000, Federal Way, WA 98093, USA.

OCP Publications, 5536 N.E. Hassalo, Portland, OR 97213, USA.

OMF International, Station Approach, Borough Green, Sevenoaks, TN15 8BG, UK.

Oxford University Press, Great Clarendon Street, Oxford, OX2 6DP, UK.

PolyGram Music Publishing Ltd, 47 British Grove, London W4, UK. *(Used by permission of Music Sales Ltd.)*

Signalgrade Ltd, 48 Chatsworth Avenue, London, SW20 8JZ, UK.

Simmonds, Clive, 22 St Michaels Road, Bedford, MK40 2LT, UK.

Smail, Mary, 151 Elm Park, London, SW2 2EE, UK.

Sound III, Elisnore House, 77 Fulham Palace Road, London, W6 8JA, UK. *(Used by permission of Music Sales Ltd.)*

Sovereign Lifestyle Music, P.O. Box 356, Leighton Buzzard, LU7 3WP, UK.
email: sovereignmusic@aol.com

Sovereign Music UK, P.O. Box 356, Leighton Buzzard, LU7 3WP, UK.
email: sovereignmusic@aol.com

Stassen, Linda, 175 Heggie Lane, Erin, TN 37061, USA.

TKO Publishing, P.O. Box 130, Hove, East Sussex, BN3 6QU.

Thankyou Music *(Adm. by worshiptogether.com songs excl. UK & Europe, adm. by Kingswaysongs.com.)* See Kingswaysongs.com.

WGRG (Wild Goose Resource Group), Iona Community, Fourth Floor, Savoy House, 140 Sauchiehall Street, Glasgow, G2 3DH.

World Wide Worship, Buxhall, Stowmarket, Suffolk, IP14 3BW, UK. *(For the UK & European territory only.)*

Index of First Lines

This index combines all the songs from the four Large Print editions, with songs from this edition highlighted in **bold**. Songs from Volume 1 (numbers 1 to 640), Volume 2 (numbers 641 to 1150) and Volume 3 (numbers 1151 to 1690) remain in normal type